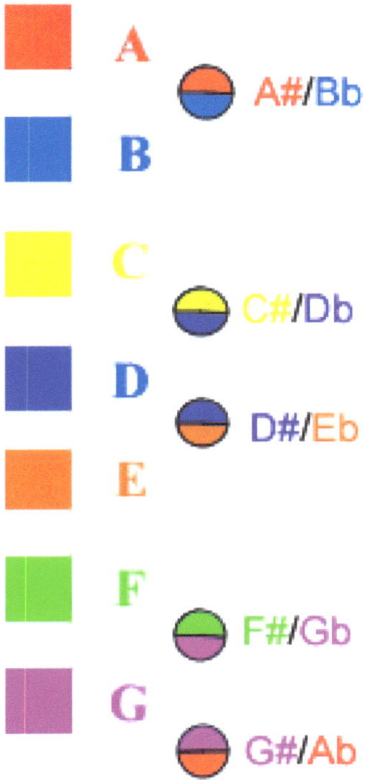

■ A
● A#/Bb

■ B

■ C
● C#/Db

■ D
● D#/Eb

■ E

■ F
● F#/Gb

■ G
● G#/Ab

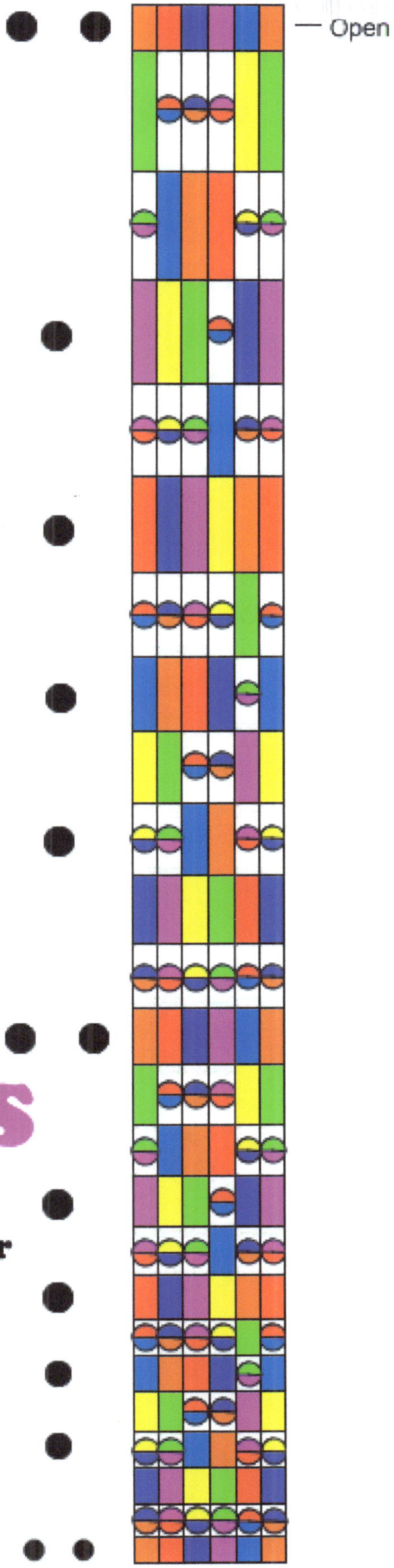

Color by Numbers

Guitar for the Visual Learner

By:

Rocco D'Ambrosca

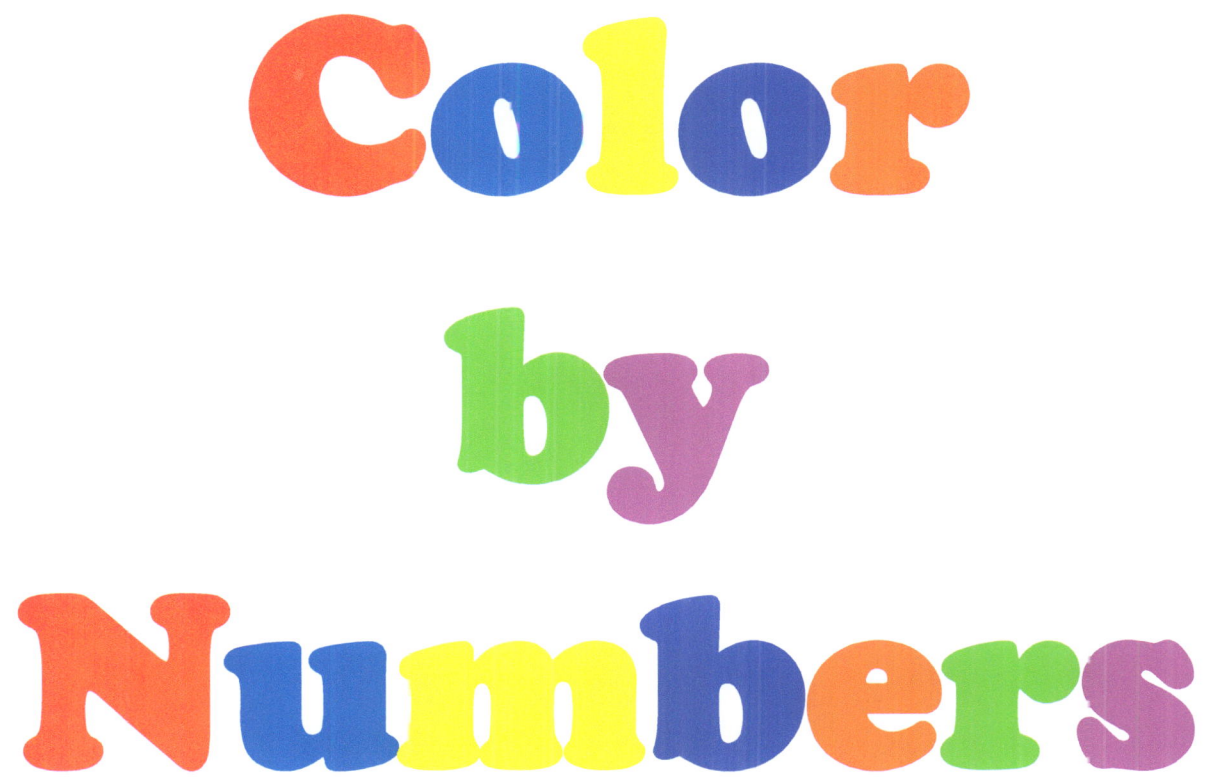

Guitar for the Visual Learner

By:

Rocco D'Ambrosca

Copyright © 2014 by Rocco Joseph D'Ambrosca

All rights reserved.

Printed in the United States of America

ISBN: 9780615993843

Dear Reader,

The only thing a teacher can do for a student is show them the possibilities. What they do in the end is up to them.

The book you have just opened offers a groundbreaking new system that teaches all basic scales and chords in a completely unique and truly revolutionary way.

After taking guitar lessons and buying several books over the years, I still wasn't progressing as I felt I should be and still wasn't the type of guitar player I wanted to be. I thought about why I really wanted to play the guitar in the first place and why I continue to play.

Besides the obvious desire to play my favorite songs, I wanted to be able to just play from myself unaccompanied. I wanted to be able to pick up any guitar and just play whatever I was thinking or feeling while having a vocabulary to draw from with which to do that.

I wanted to be able to play the guitar fretboard as freely and effortlessly as a computer keyboard, being able to string notes together into melodies the way I can string letters into words and phrases without having to do anything but think it and allow my fingers to do the rest simply by reflex.

Conceptually, I could understand that melody, words, phrases, letters, and musical notes, were so synonymous with each other that if I could simply master the musical alphabet and vocabulary of the guitar, I would finally be on the path to being the guitar player I had always wanted to be.

I set forth to memorize this musical vocabulary of scales and chords, working towards their mastery through a series of focused exercises that I came to develop, using a revolutionary new method of reading and diagraming scales and chords on the guitar fretboard, for both ease of memorization and depth of musical understanding.

All of this combined has given me incredible playing ability, great depth in my musical knowledge, and an intuitive understanding of the instrument. This has all been of great use to me as a songwriter, performer, and mentor to friends.

I hope to share this same knowledge with you.

Sincerely,

Rocco D'Ambrosca

Contents

- **Introduction** — 1
- **Scales Introduction** — 3
- **Chromatic Scale** — 9
- **Standard Scale Box Patterns** — 10
- **Standard Major/Minor Scales** — 12
- **Pentatonic Scale Box Patterns** — 24
- **Pentatonic Major/Minor Scales** — 26

- **Chords Introduction** — 38
- **Movable Chord Shapes** — 40
- **Major Chords** — 44
- **Minor Chords** — 58
- **Dominant 7th Chords** — 71
- **Major 7th Chords** — 86
- **Minor 7th Chords** — 92

-Introduction-

Ever play Battleship?

The game of Battleship is played using a grid based system to call out shots on your opponent's grid, trying to hit a point that contains a section on one of your opponent's ships.

When I saw the fretboard of a guitar neck with the strings running from end to end, I saw a grid. Before my hands ever touched a guitar, I already knew how to play one.

I immediately understood that playing notes in a scale would just come down to knowing what points on the grid of frets and strings to hit in sequence. Chords would then follow to just be hitting multiple points on the grid together at the same time.

From the moment I owned a guitar and started playing, I knew that what I had to do was learn all the notes of scales on the guitar's fretboard as points on a grid played individually and all chords on the guitar's fretboard as groups of points on a grid played together.

Color by Numbers

The title of this book comes from the pages in children's activity books often called or referred to as color by numbers.

On these "color by number" pages, you would find a picture scene with various outlined sections numbered, with a different color corresponding to each number. Several sections may be numbered the same, meaning that all these sections would be colored in with the same color. By following along with the number to color key listed on the page, and coloring in each numbered section with the correct color, the picture scene would come to life with proper complexion and detail.

By combing this color by number concept with the grid concept from the game battleship, the full reality and potential of the Color by Numbers Guitar System comes into focus.

The Color by Numbers Guitar System

I realized that all the chord books and scale books I bought or looked through at the store, lacked any true system to put all of it together in an easy to understand way or in a way that would be easily memorable or truly integrated as a whole.

I decided to create my own system that would unite both the notes of scales and the notes of chords into a truly integrated, easily memorable, and extremely easily understood system.

I went ahead and assigned every note a color. All natural notes would be given solid colors and all sharp/flat notes would be given a circle colored each half of its corresponding natural notes:

A is red, A#/Bb is red/blue, B is blue, C is yellow, C#/Db is yellow/purple, D is purple, D#/Eb is purple/orange, E is orange, F is green, F#/Gb is green/pink, G is pink, and G#/Ab is pink/red.

Once every note had an assigned color, I created a grid of six columns, one for each string, with a total of twenty-five rows, one for each fret of a 24 fret guitar, plus an extra row at the top for the open tuning of each string.

Each box or section point, on this six column by twenty-five row grid, would represent a note on the fretboard of the guitar. Each note position would simply be the combination of two numbers, the column or string number and the corresponding row or fret number.

Once I had this basic color coded grid system in place, I began using it to create chord and scale diagrams by translating traditionally available chord and scale books into this new color coded grid based system.

In each diagram, every note included in a chord or scale, is shown as being both colored its assigned color shade and placed in its proper position on the grid in respect to both string and fret position. All chord and scale diagrams in this new system would now show both proper note position and composition of every chord and scale diagramed.

Just a single glance at any chord or scale diagram in this book, will instantly tell you what notes are used by color and in what positions those notes fall upon the natural grid structure of strings and frets on the guitar neck.

The Language of Music

Music is a language. Like any language you learn, the most basic and fundamental starting point is to learn the alphabet and vocabulary of the language. When it comes to the language of music, think of musical notes as the alphabet that gives you the basic building blocks for the entire foundation and construction of the language. As with every language, this alphabet of musical notes is used to create a vocabulary to communicate with. This alphabet of musical notes makes up the vocabulary of scales and chords in the musical language. Once known, this vocabulary of scales and chords allows you to begin speaking the language of music.

At first, speaking is largely limited to repeating what is said by others just as a baby repeats the phrases spoken by their parents and others around them. In music, this means listening to and playing the songs of other musicians. As more songs are learned, the grammar and usage of the musical vocabulary is slowly understood. The language is learned from understanding how other speakers use the vocabulary of that language to communicate. By seeing and understanding how other musicians speak using the vocabulary of the musical language, you learn how to speak the language of music just as you learned your own native language. Just as all authors learn to write from reading the written works of other authors, you will learn to write and play your own music by listening, playing and studying the music of other musicians.

-Scales Introduction-

The Musical Alphabet/Chromatic Scale

The alphabet of musical notes is made up of the twelve notes or pitches in the Chromatic scale, A, A#/Bb, B, C, C#/Db, D, D#/Eb, E, F, F#/Gb, G, G#/Ab.

A, B, C, D, E, F, and G are known as naturals, with A#/Bb, C#/Db, D#/Eb, F#/Gb, and G#/Ab known as accidentals, placed in order alphabetically between they're corresponding natural notes. Since these accidentals fall in between the place of two natural notes, they are named based on these natural notes. Each accidental note is both the sharp (#) or flat (b) of the note above or below it in pitch along the Chromatic scale. This is why the note between A and B natural is called both A# and Bb.

The determining factor of whether an accidental note is written or read as a sharp or flat is based on the key of music being played. The most important thing is to understand they represent the same pitch and fretboard note position.

<u>Key Concept:</u> The basic building blocks of an alphabet are the parts used in countless variations and combinations of construction. Using just a simple base set of parts you can create infinite variations of complex constructions. Like the base set of atomic elements used to create infinite variations of molecules and combinations of molecules, the notes of the musical alphabet serve as the base set of elements used to create the scales and chords of the musical language.

The Chromatic scale is the most basic fundamental scale. The twelve notes of the chromatic scale are used as the foundational building blocks to create all other scales and chords. Each of the twelve notes is separated equally in spacing within the chromatic scale. On the fretboard it is the distance of a single fret along the length of the guitar neck, also known as a half-step. This half-step distance is the same as any two keys placed side by side on a piano keyboard. This scale pattern of half-step spacing repeats again and again, in alphabetic order starting from any note, in either ascending or descending direction to create the chromatic scale.

Every string on the guitar can therefore be considered as a Chromatic scale, ascending in pitch by moving up each fret on the neck towards the body of the guitar and descending in pitch moving away from the body, back down the neck. The relative pitch heard when hitting a string is determined by the length of the string vibrating. As your finger is placed on a fret closer towards the body of the guitar, the length of the string allowed to vibrate becomes shorter and shorter, creating a higher pitch. The note heard when playing a string without placing your finger on any fret is called playing an open note or open string.

By tuning a guitar to standard tuning, your guitar's open notes will be: E, A, D, G, B, E, as listed in order from thickest to thinnest string gauge. Each string goes up one note in the Chromatic scale for each fret along the guitar's neck, repeating each string's open note at the twelfth fret, and again at the twenty-fourth. This repeating of the open note at the twelfth fret, and again at the twenty-fourth fret is known as an octave.

Scale Vocabulary: Chromatic Scale

The definition of a scale is an organization of notes. Scales have a set number of notes placed in order with a specific spacing between each note to create a repeating pattern.

The Chromatic scale is considered the most basic and fundamental scale because it includes all the notes of the musical alphabet without any variation in note spacing. All other scales and chords are formed from a variation in the notes included and the spacing between them. This variation of included notes and note spacing is what gives each scale and chord their own distinct sound.

The Chromatic scale, like all scales, starts, stops, and repeats from a root note, with each repetition of the scale pattern being another octave of that scale. This root note is also referred to as the key of the scale and is most important in referencing the musical key of a specific melody, song, or piece of music. No matter which root note or key you decide to use in the chromatic scale, every other note to follow will be a single fret or half-step away, until returning back to the root note again at a higher or lower octave. The Chromatic scale therefore uses every note in the musical alphabet no matter which root note/musical key you decide to use because there is never a possibility of skipping over any notes along the way through the scale, due to the equal spacing pattern and twelve note requirements that define the Chromatic scale.

Other scales have fewer notes, but have note spacing patterns more complex than the all equal spacing of the Chromatic scale. This variation in note spacing causes some notes in the musical alphabet to be skipped over so that the notes included vary from scale to scale and key to key. Since this variation does not exist in the Chromatic scale, all notes in the musical alphabet available on the guitar are included in the Chromatic scale and there is no variation from key to key. Therefore, only one fretboard diagram is required to display the Chromatic scale as seen on the front cover.

Scale Vocabulary: Standard Scale

As stated before, each scale is defined by the number of notes included and the interval pattern between these notes. A scale starts on a root note, counts off notes through the musical alphabet as defined by the interval pattern, ends with that same root note an octave higher, and then continues on repeating again and again.

The spacing intervals used in interval patterns consist of half steps (H) and whole steps (W). A half-step equals the distance of a single fret along the fretboard, while a whole step equals the distance of two frets along the fretboard. The notes of a scale are numbered as degrees, starting with a root note as the first degree and then numbering a degree for each note included in the interval pattern. The Chromatic scale for example, includes twelve notes/degrees separated by an interval pattern consisting of all half-steps.

The most common and widely used scale, used in almost every style of music, including classical, opera, theater, cinema, cartoons, jazz, pop, rock, metal, and rap, is the Major and Minor Standard scale.

The Major Standard scale is best known as the scale introduced to children as: Do, Re, Mi, Fa, Sol, La, Ti, Do. The Major and Minor Standard scale are also simply known as the Major and Minor scale, but are referred to as the Major and Minor Standard scale in this book for both differentiation and emphasis of importance above all other Major and Minor scales.

<u>Key Concept:</u> The Standard Scale's greatest importance is serving as the foundational basis for other scales and chords, which will be discussed later.

The Standard scale includes seven notes with a Major scale interval pattern of W, W, H, W, W, W, H. Every Major scale has a corresponding relative Minor scale. This relative Minor scale uses both the same notes and interval pattern as its relative Major scale, but starts the interval pattern from a different note so that the first note of a relative Minor scale has the sixth note of its relative Major scale.

By using the Major scale interval pattern of W, W, H, W, W, W, H, we get the Minor scale interval pattern by repeating this same pattern, but starting on the sixth note or scale degree of the pattern resulting with, W, H, W, W, H, W, W. In this way the Major and Minor scales are relative to each other.

Major interval pattern repeated: W, W, H, W, W, W, H, W, W, H, W, W, W, H,
                                     1, 2, 3, 4, 5, 6, 7, 1, 2, 3, 4, 5, 6, 7,

    Starting from the sixth degree.   /\

        Minor interval pattern: W, H, W, W, H, W, W,

Major Scale Degrees:	1, 2, 3, 4, 5, 6, 7, 1, 2, 3, 4, 5, 6, 7, 1
C Major Standard:	C, D, E, F, G, A, B, C, D, E, F, G, A, B, C
A Minor Standard:	A, B, C, D, E, F, G, A, B, C, D, E, F, G, A
Minor Scale Degrees:	1, 2, 3, 4, 5, 6, 7, 1, 2, 3, 4, 5, 6, 7, 1,

Scale Vocabulary: Standard Scale Continued...

To further examine the relationship between scale pattern intervals and relative major and minor scales, we will use the scales of C Chromatic, C Major Standard, and A Minor Standard as examples.

(As stated before, each scale is defined by the number of notes included and the interval spacing pattern between these notes. The Chromatic scale includes twelve notes separated by all half-steps.)

Using C as our root note, we get the C Chromatic scale by counting off twelve notes through the musical alphabet starting from C and not skipping any notes so that they are all a half-step apart.

Musical alphabet: A, A#, B, C, C#, D, D#, E, F, F#, G, G#, A...
      C Chromatic: C, C#, D, D#, E, F, F#, G, G#, A, A#, B, C

Using C as our root note again, we get the C Major scale by counting off eight notes through the musical alphabet starting from C and skipping over a few notes with whole steps where defined by the Major interval pattern.

Musical alphabet: A, A#, B, C, C#, D, D#, E, F, F#, G, G#, A...

Major interval pattern: W, W, H, W, W, W, H

C, W-step, D, W-step, E, H-step, F, W-step, G, W-step, A, W-step, B, H-step, C.

C, skip C#, D, skip D#, E, H-step, F, skip F#, G, skip G#, A, skip A#, B, H-step, C.

C Major Standard: C, D, E, F, G, A, B, C

Finally, using A as our root note, we get the A Minor Scale by counting off eight notes through the musical alphabet starting from A and skipping over a few notes with whole steps where defined by the Minor interval pattern.

Musical alphabet: A, A#, B, C, C#, D, D#, E, F, F#, G, G#, A...

Minor interval pattern: W, H, W, W, H, W, W

A, W-step, B, H-step, C, W-step, D, W-step, E, H-step, F, W-step, G, W-step, A.

A, skip A#, B, H-step, C, skip C#, D, skip D#, E, H-step, F, skip G#, G, skip G#, A.

A Minor Standard: A, B, C, D, E, F, G, A

The table below illustrates this special relationship between relative Major and Minor scales, specifically the same notes and interval pattern using C Major Standard and A Minor Standard Scales as examples.

Major Interval Pattern: W, W, H, W, W, W, H   Minor Interval Pattern: W, H, W, W, H, W, W
C Major Scale Degrees: 1, 2, 3, 4, 5, 6, 7, 1   A Minor Scale Degrees: 1, 2, 3, 4, 5, 6, 7, 1
C Major Scale Notes: C, D, E, F, G, A, B, C   A Minor Scale Notes: A, B, C, D, E, F, G, A
Major Scale: Do, Re, Mi, Fa, Sol, La, Ti, Do   Minor Scale: La, Ti, Do, Re, Mi, Fa, Sol, La

Looking at the table, we see:

- The Minor scale interval pattern to be the same as the Major scale interval pattern but started from the sixth degree of the Major scale interval pattern.
- The A Minor scale to be the same as the C Major scale but started from the sixth degree of the C Major scale.
- The Minor scale to be the same as the Major scale but started from the sixth degree of the Major scale.

This next table lists all relative Major and Minor scales:

C Major   = A Minor
C#/Db Major   = A#/Bb Minor
D Major   = B Minor
D#/Eb Major   = C Minor
E Major   = C#/Db Minor
F Major   = D Minor
F#/Gb Major   = D#/Eb Minor
G Major   = E Minor
G#/Ab Major   = F Minor
A Major   = F#/Gb Minor
A#/Bb Major   = G Minor
B Major   = G#/Ab Minor

Scale Vocabulary: Pentatonic Scale

The Pentatonic scale is most commonly used in Blues, Folk, Country, and Rock.

(As mentioned before, the notes of a scale are numbered as degrees, starting with a root note as the first degree and then numbering a degree for each note included in the interval pattern.)

The Pentatonic scale includes five notes taken from the scale degrees of the Standard scale.

While the Standard scale includes seven notes, the Pentatonic uses only five of those notes.

The Major Standard scale degrees of: 1, 2, 3, 5, and 6 form the Major Pentatonic scale.
The Minor Standard scale degrees of: 1, 3, 4, 5, and 7 form the Minor Pentatonic scale.

C Major Standard Scale Degrees:	1, 2, 3, 4, 5, 6, 7, 1
C Major Standard Scale Notes:	C, D, E, F, G, A, B, C
C Major Pentatonic Scale Degrees:	1, 2, 3, 5, 6, 1
C Major Pentatonic Scale Notes:	C, D, E, G, A, C
A Minor Standard Scale Degrees:	1, 2, 3, 4, 5, 6, 7, 1
A Minor Standard Scale Notes:	A, B, C, D, E, F, G, A
A Minor Pentatonic Scale Degrees:	1, 3, 4, 5, 7, 1
A Minor Pentatonic Scale Notes:	A, C, D, E, G, A

(This basis of other scales and chords, using Standard scale degrees is the most overwhelming reason this book refers to the Standard scale as the Standard scale.)

Scale Vocabulary: Box Patterns

On the guitar, the easiest way to memorize each scale is by using what are known as box patterns.

Box patterns are an organization of notes, grouped together in a specific arrangement based on scale type. Each scale type will therefore have its own specific set of box patterns based on the variation of note spacing in that scale.

<u>Key Concept:</u> Once the box patterns of a particular scale are known, the scale is known in every possible key variation. Each key uses the same set of box patterns, with the root notes designating the key. All you need to do to change key is shift the box pattern series into position along the fretboard so that the root notes lock into the designated key you seek to play.

Although a scale extends across the entire fretboard length of the guitar's neck, up and down and across each fret and string of the guitar, box patterns break up grid sections of the fretboard into chunks of 4 or 5 frets at a time. Each of these grid chunks of frets is called a box pattern because you are boxing in or limiting your view to only a section of the entire scale length.

Each box pattern is made up of half of the box pattern before and after it. When looking at the fretboard of the guitar neck, each box pattern of frets connects into the next box pattern, so that the bottom of one pattern is the top of the next pattern to come in the repeating order of box patterns along the length of the guitar neck.

Each box pattern interlocks into the next so that the bottom frets of box pattern 1 are used as the top frets of box pattern 2, the bottom frets of box pattern 2 are used as the top frets of box pattern 3, the bottom frets of box pattern 3 are used as the top frets of box pattern 4, the bottom frets of box pattern 4 are used as the top frets of box pattern 5, the bottom frets of box pattern 5 are used as the top frets of box pattern 1, and then repeating on until you run out of frets on the fretboard.

Key Concept: Since the Pentatonic Scale is derived from the Standard Scale, both the box pattern series numbers and root note positions of each scale type are shared as a basic foundation.

-Chromatic Scale-

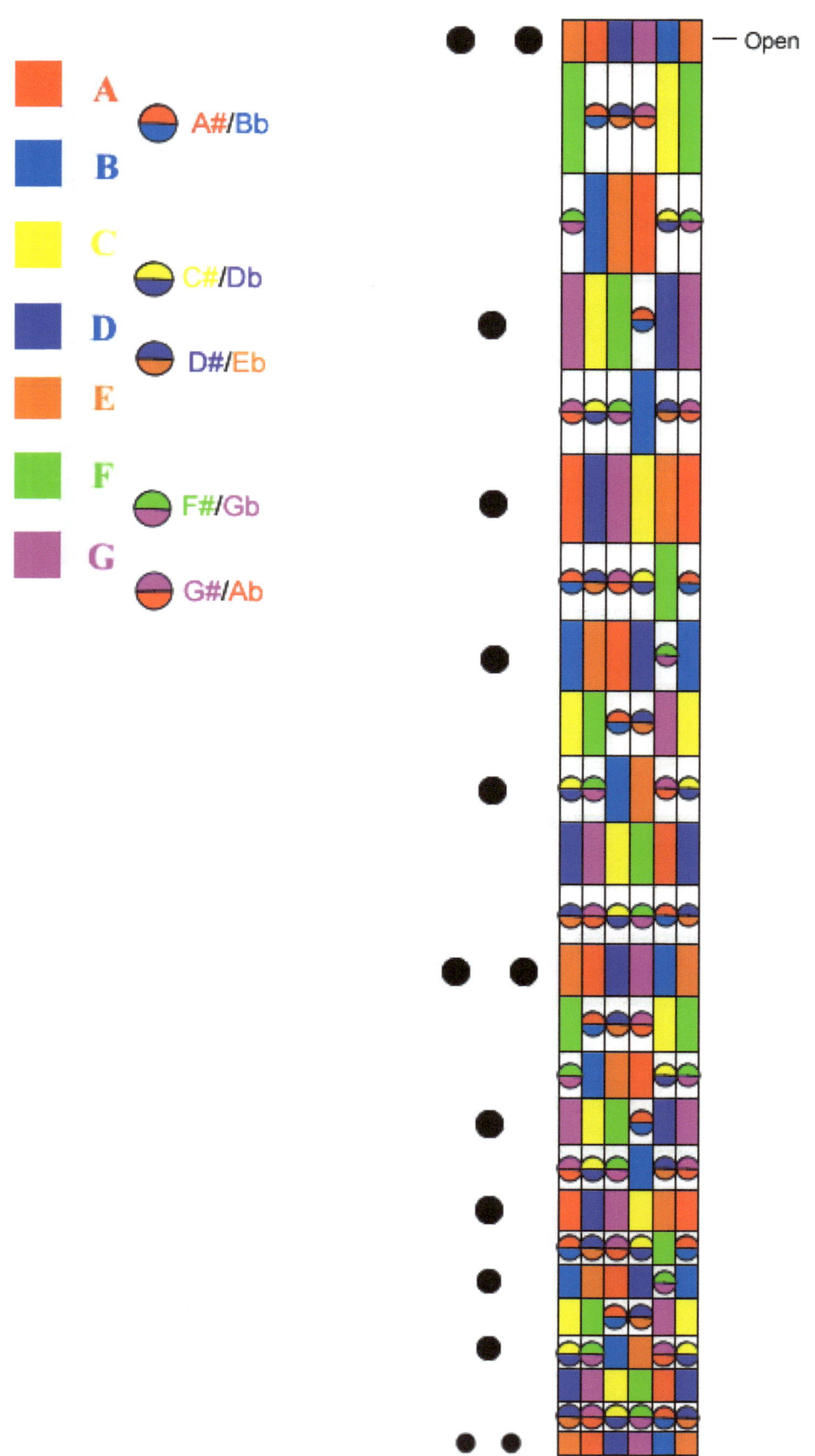

-Standard Scale Box Patterns-

Major Standard Scale Box Patterns

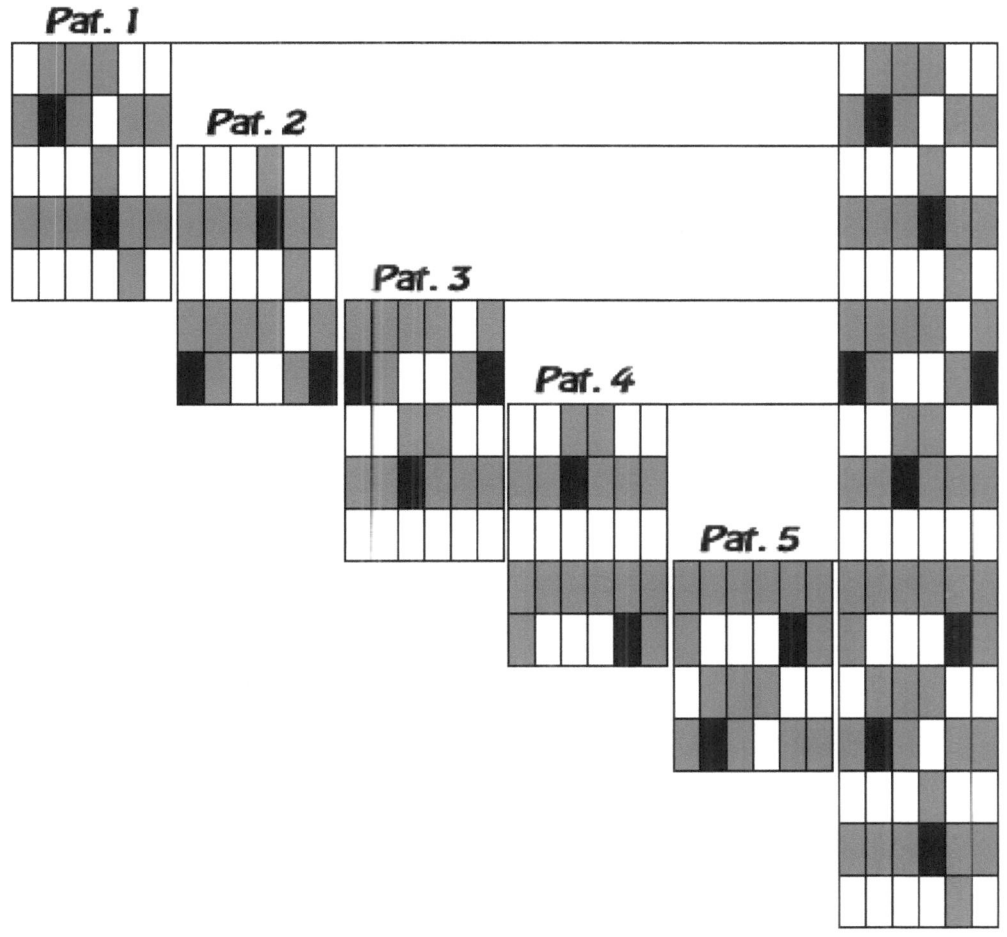

- ▩ A **Note** in the scale
- ■ A **Root Note** in the scale

Minor Standard Scale Box Patterns

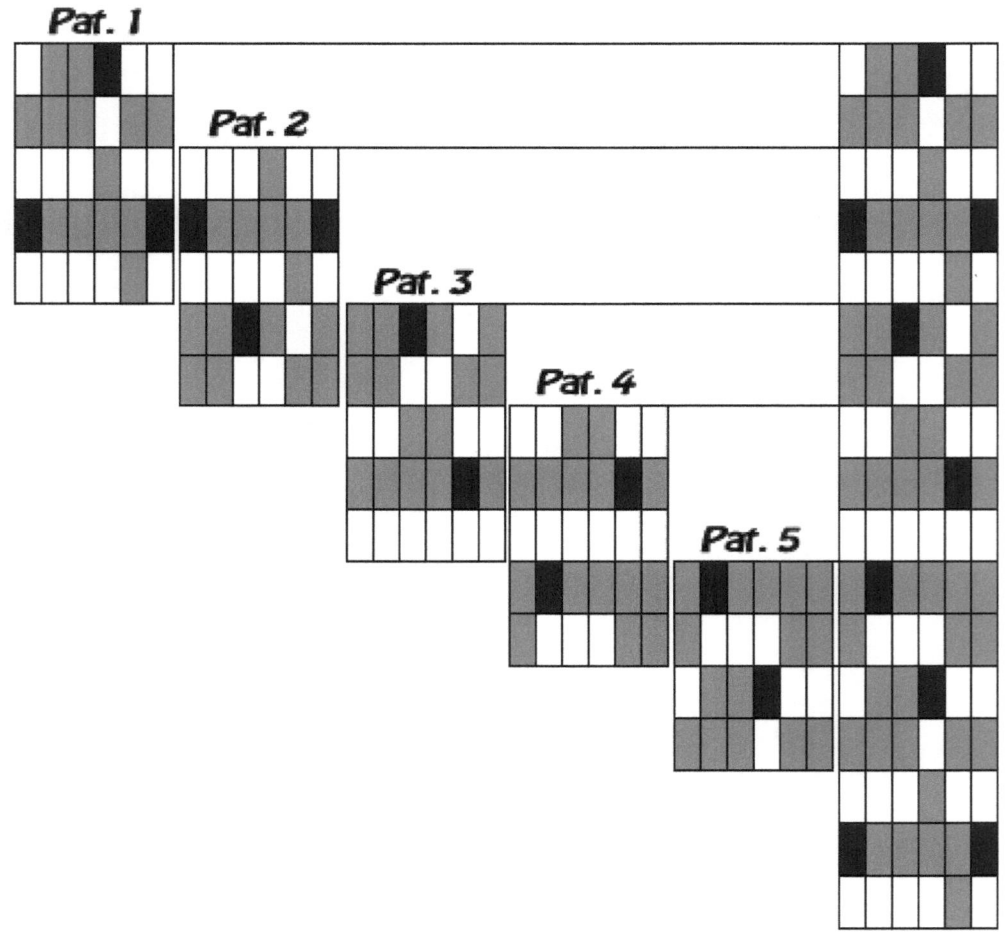

■ – A **_Note_** in the scale

■ – A **_Root Note_** in the scale

-Standard Major/Minor Scales-

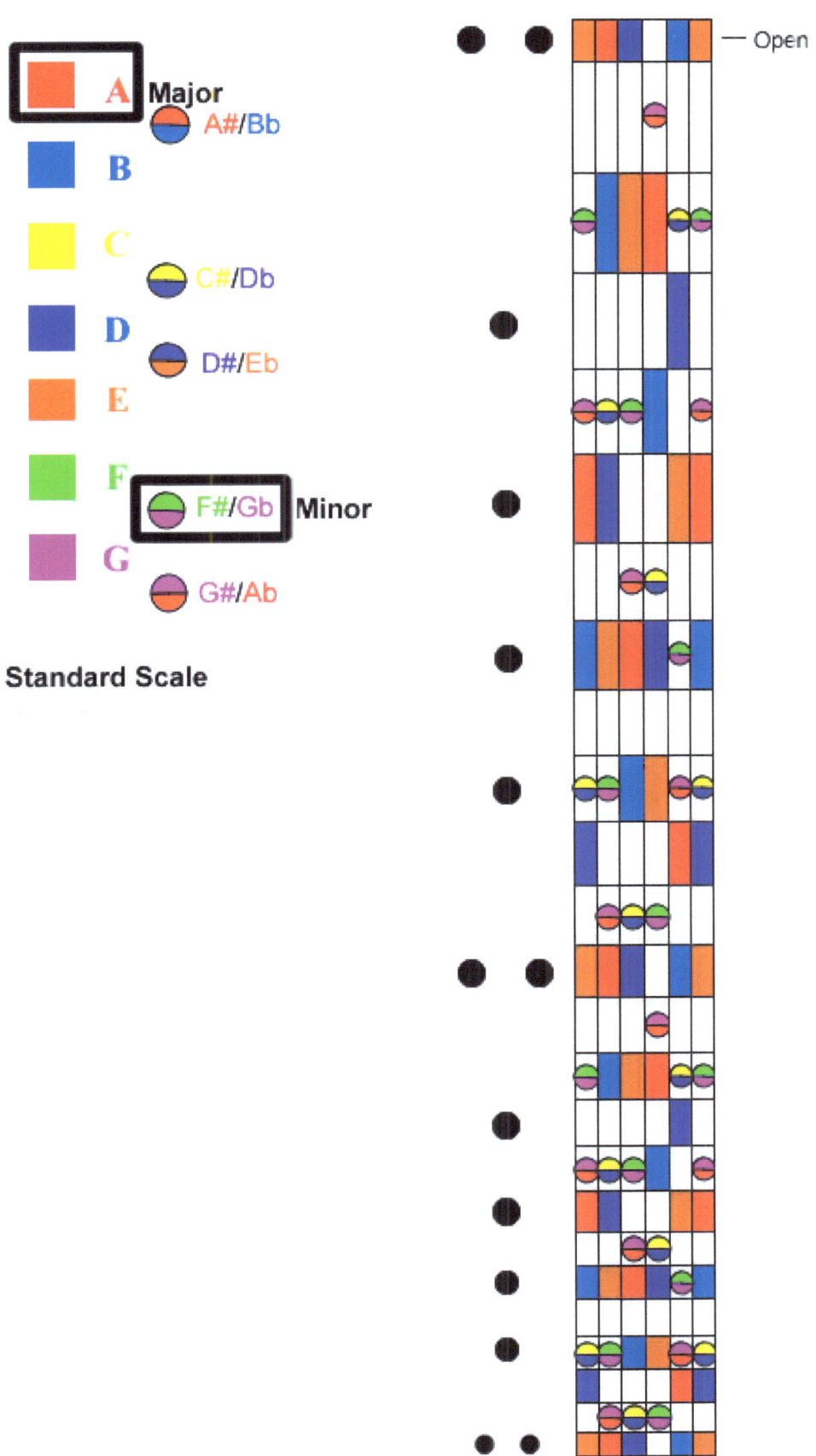

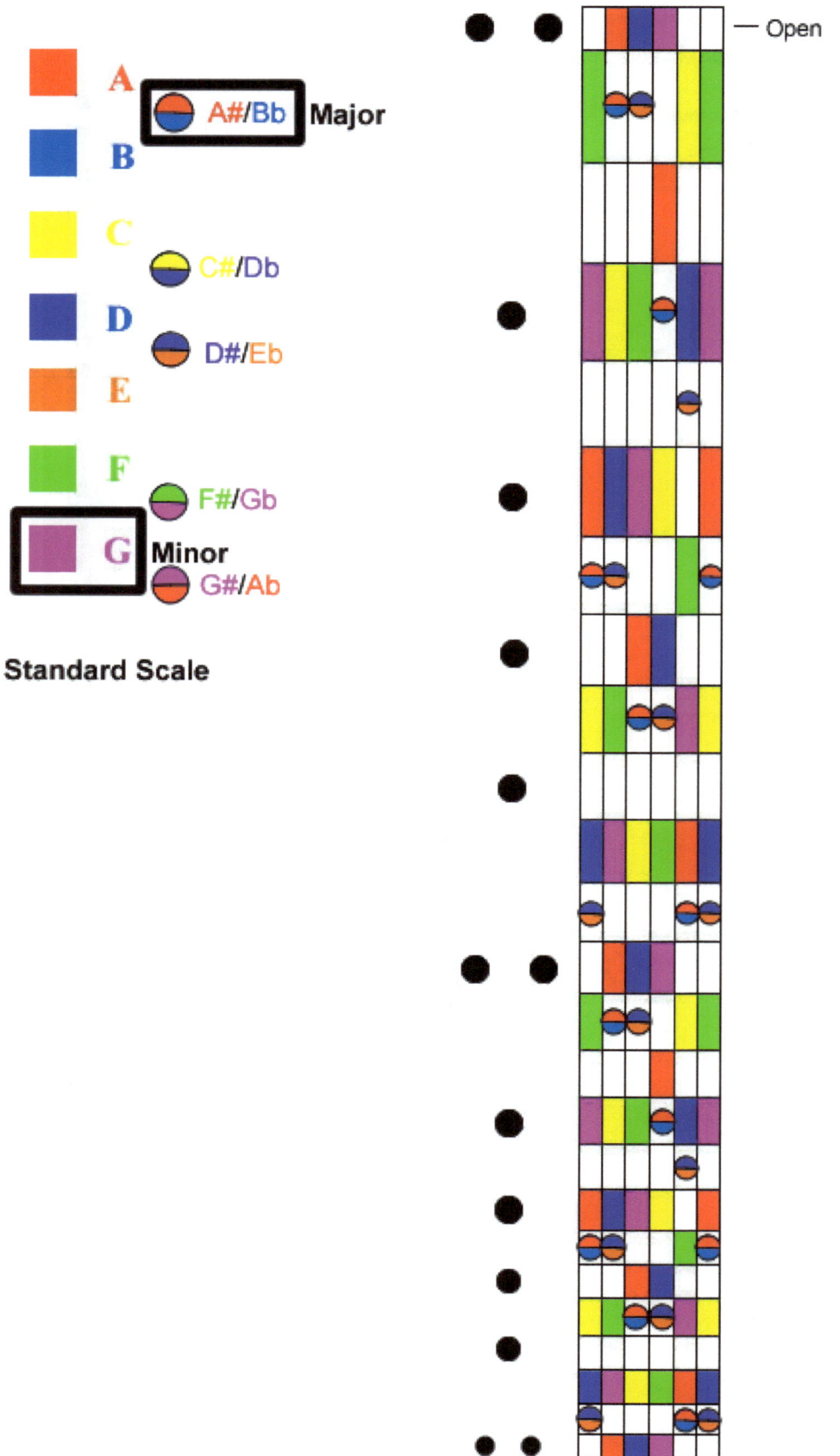

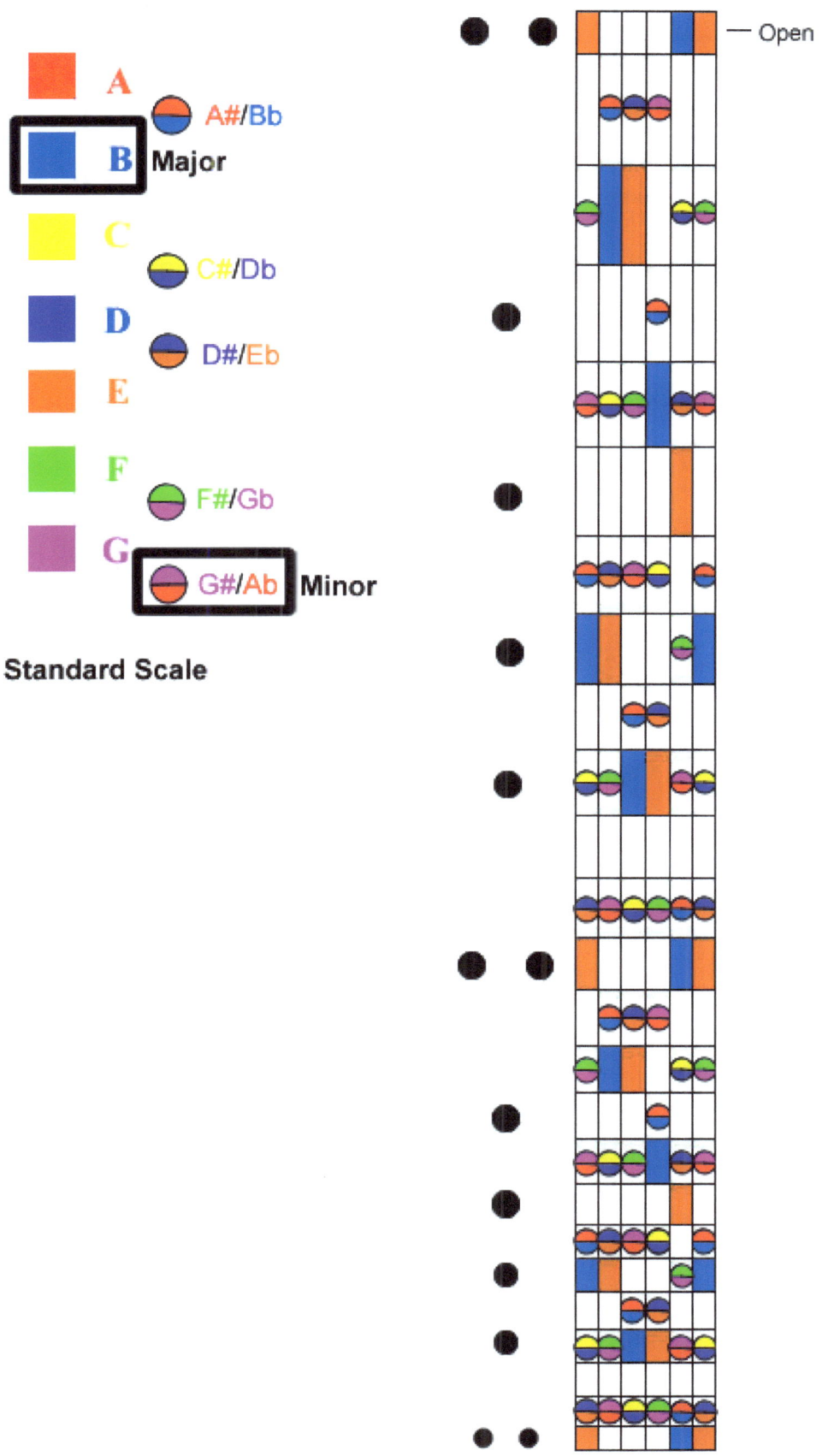

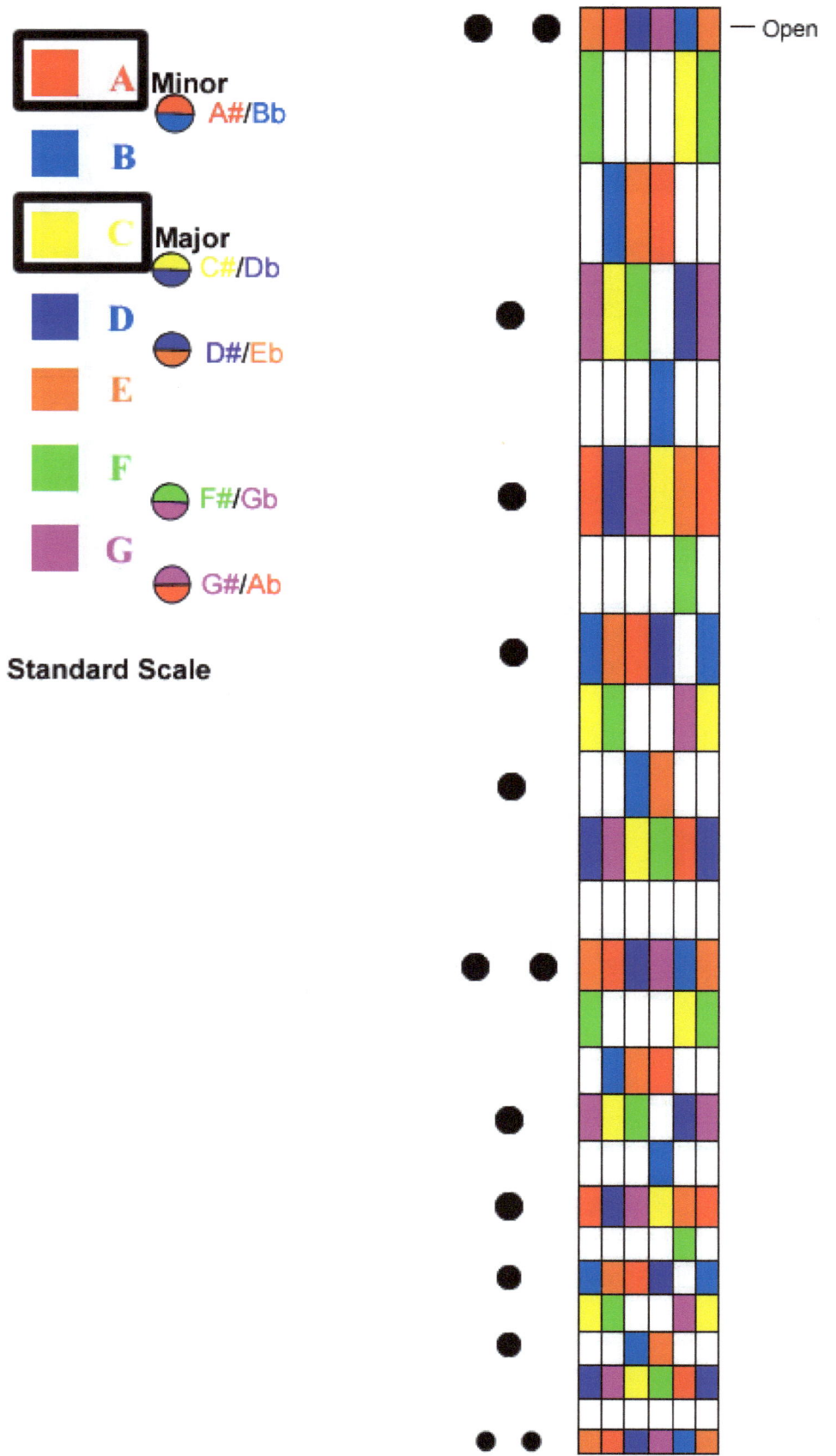

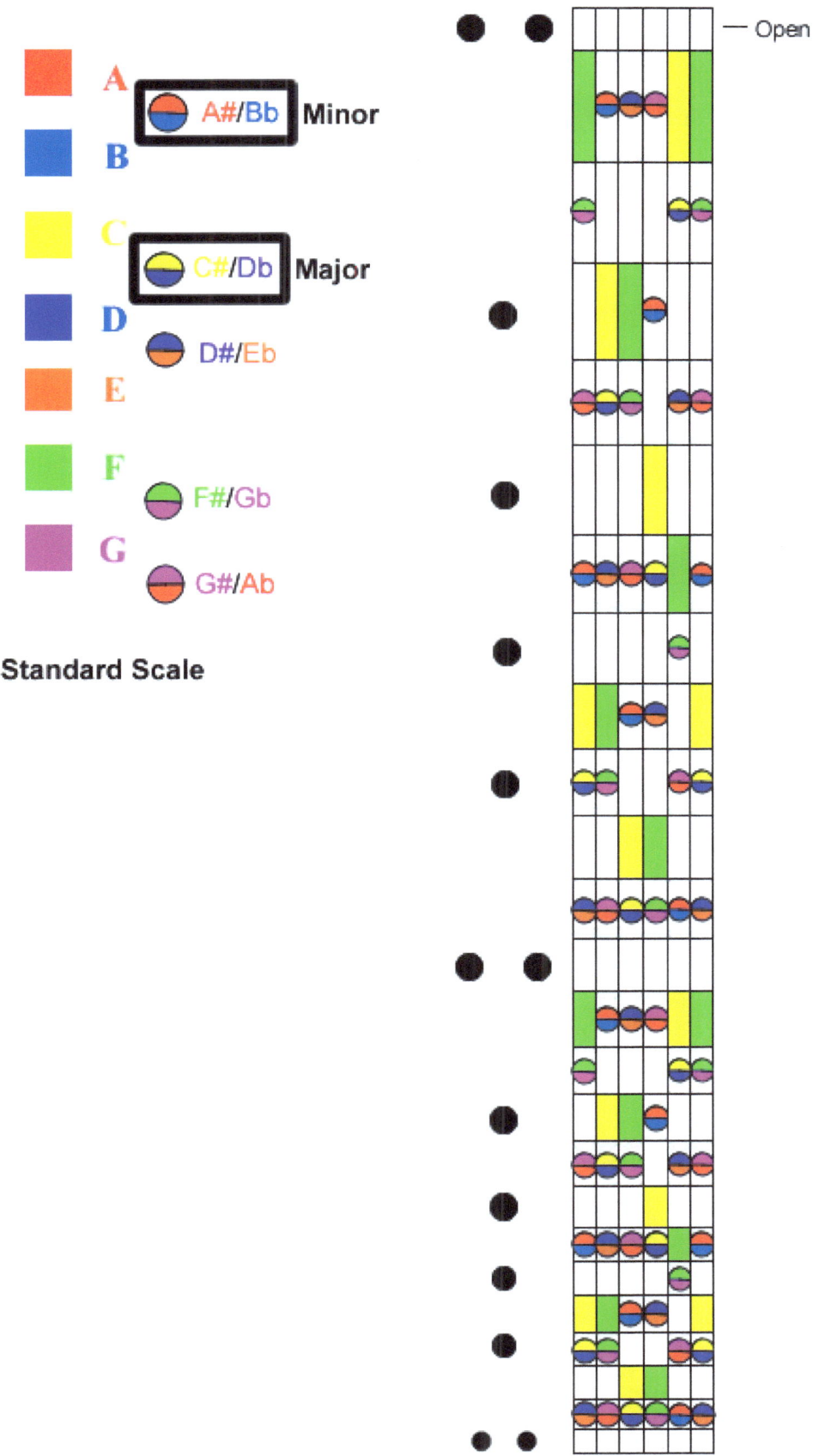

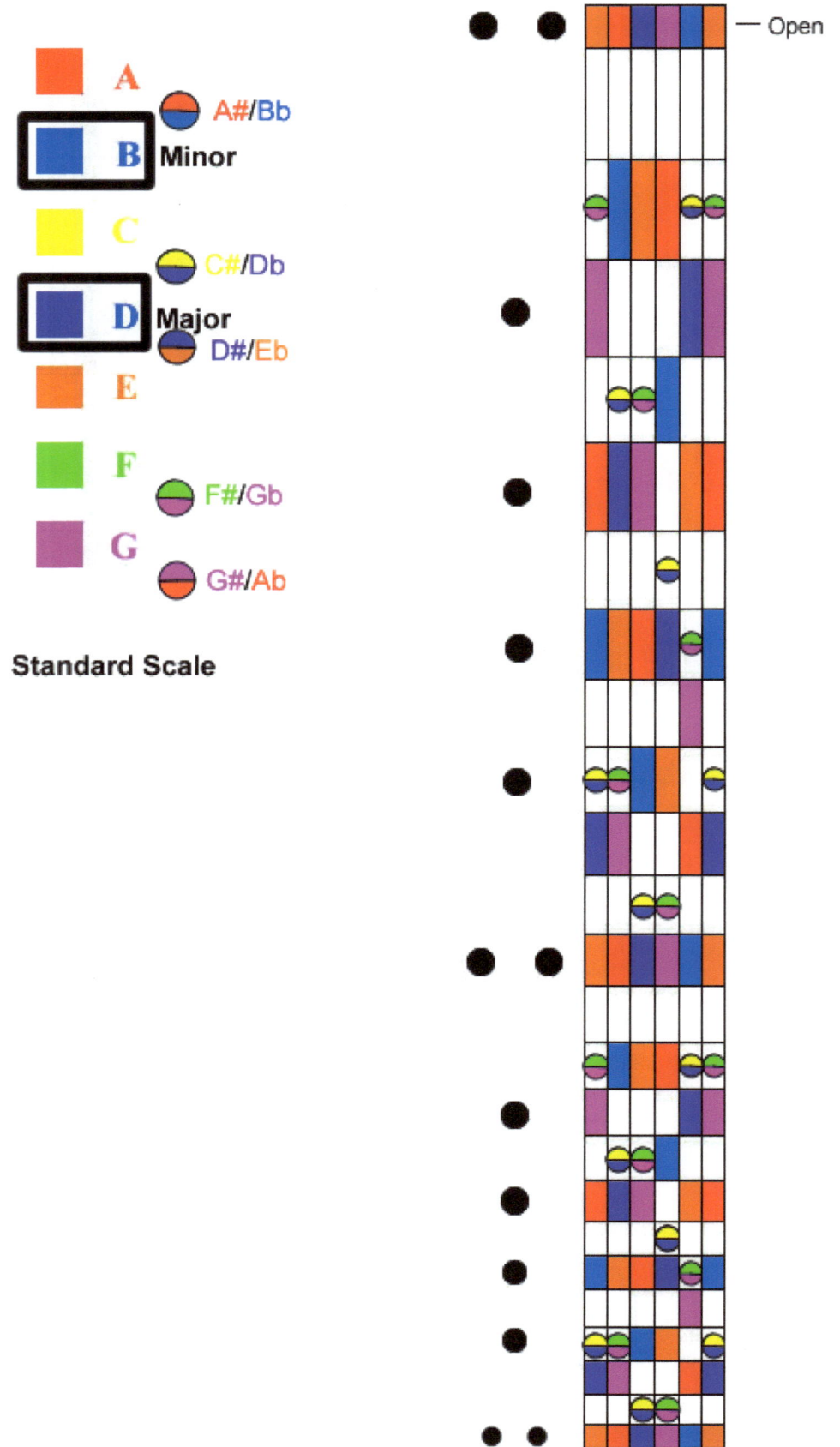

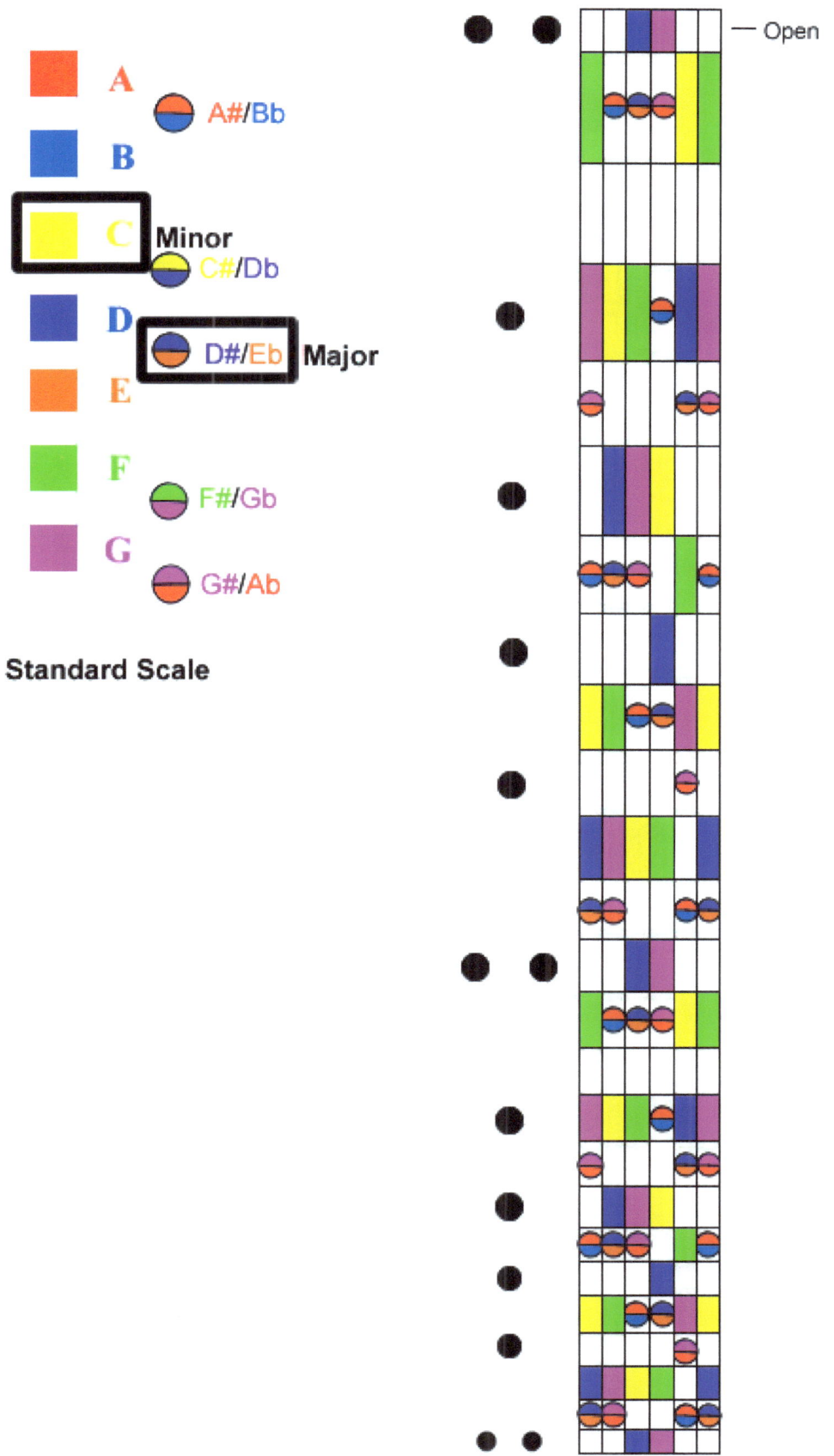

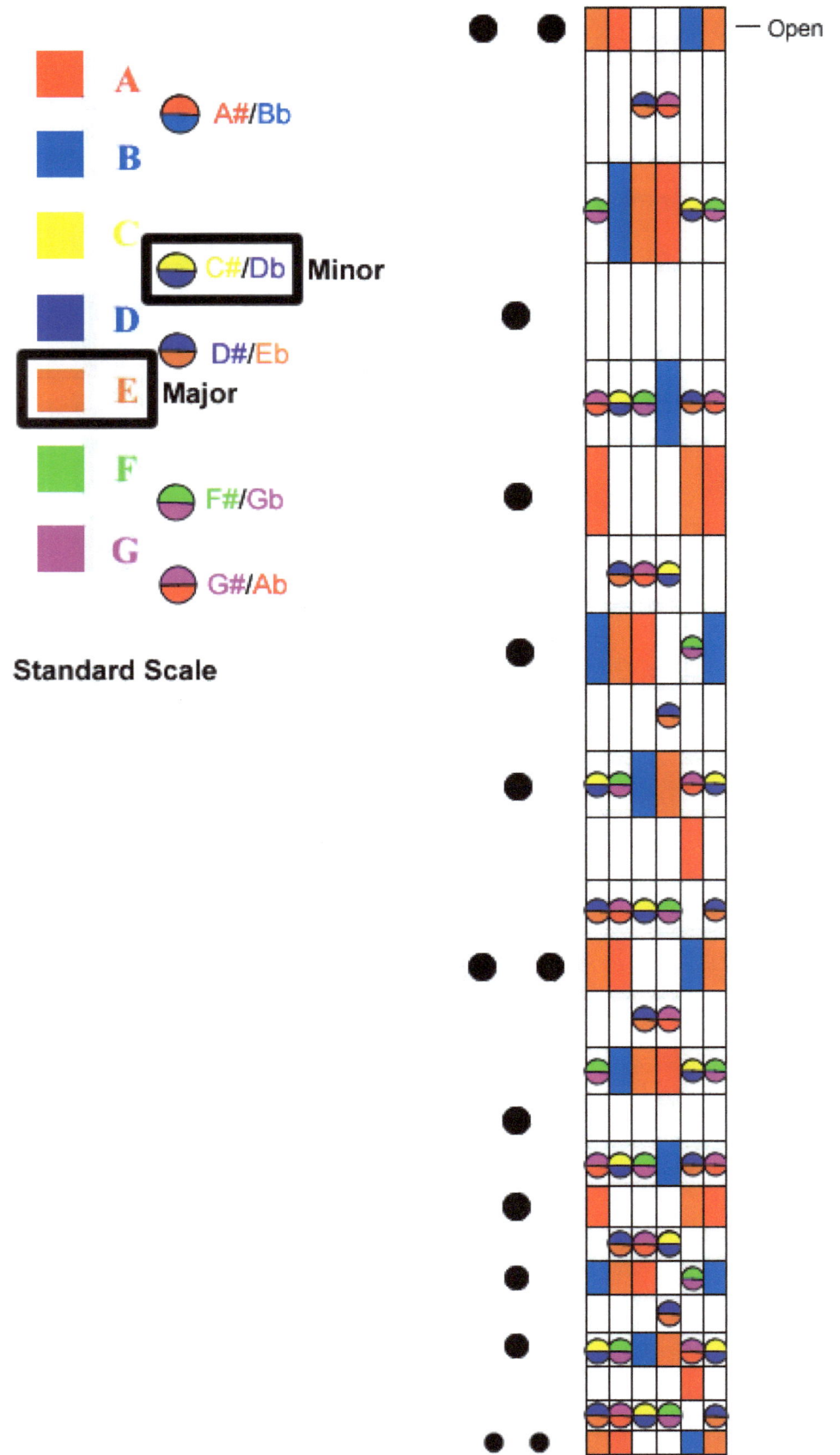

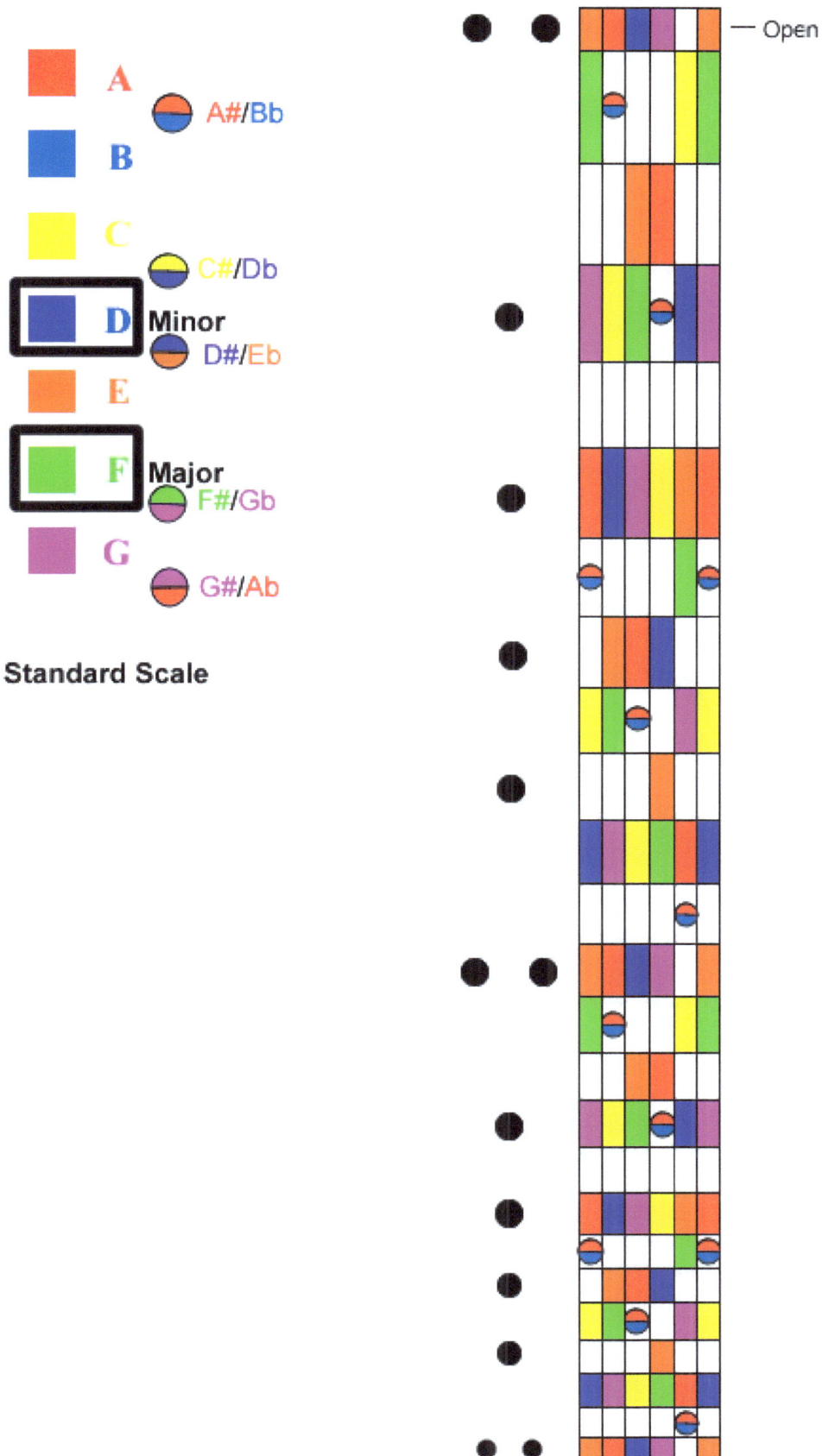

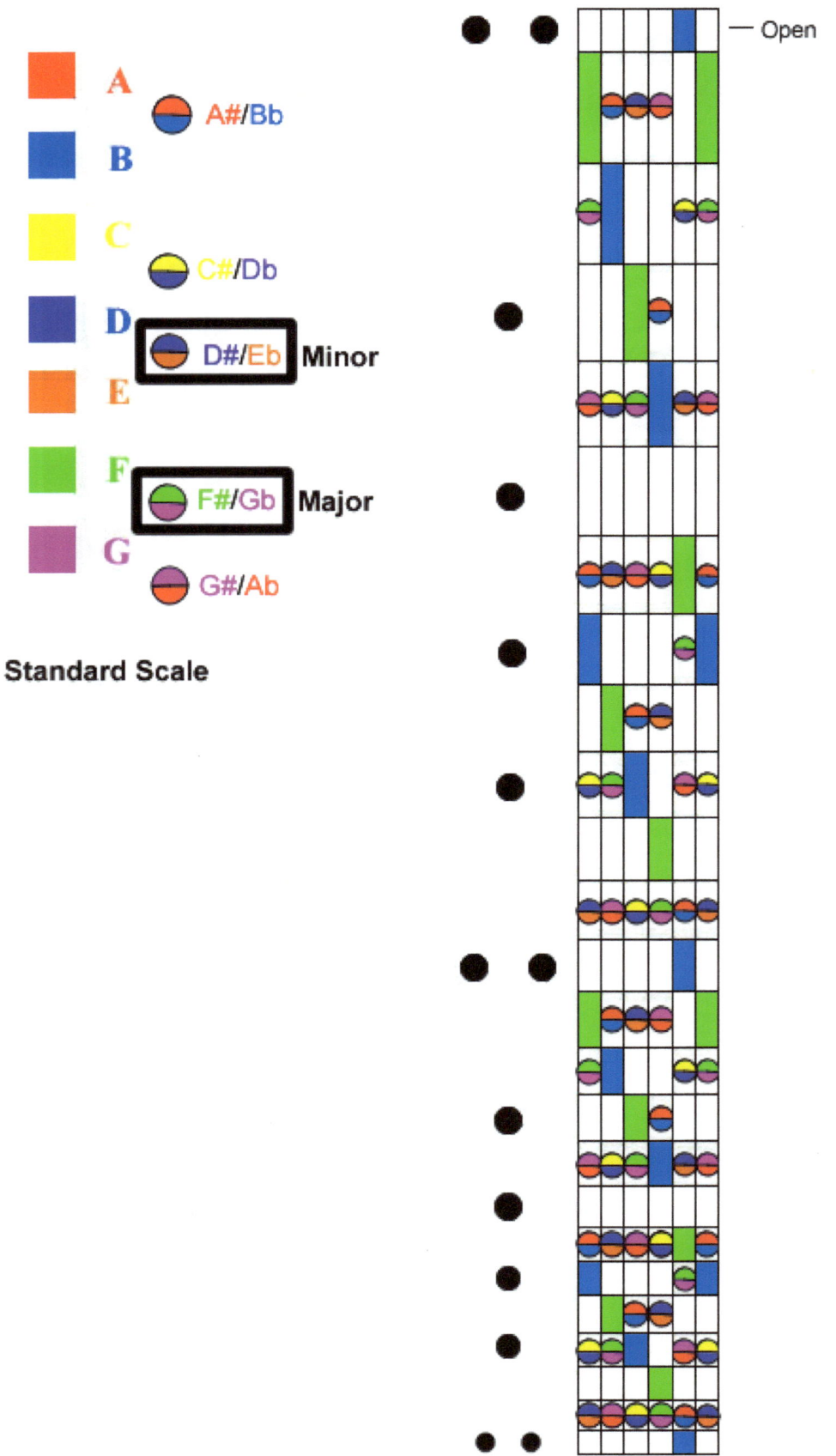

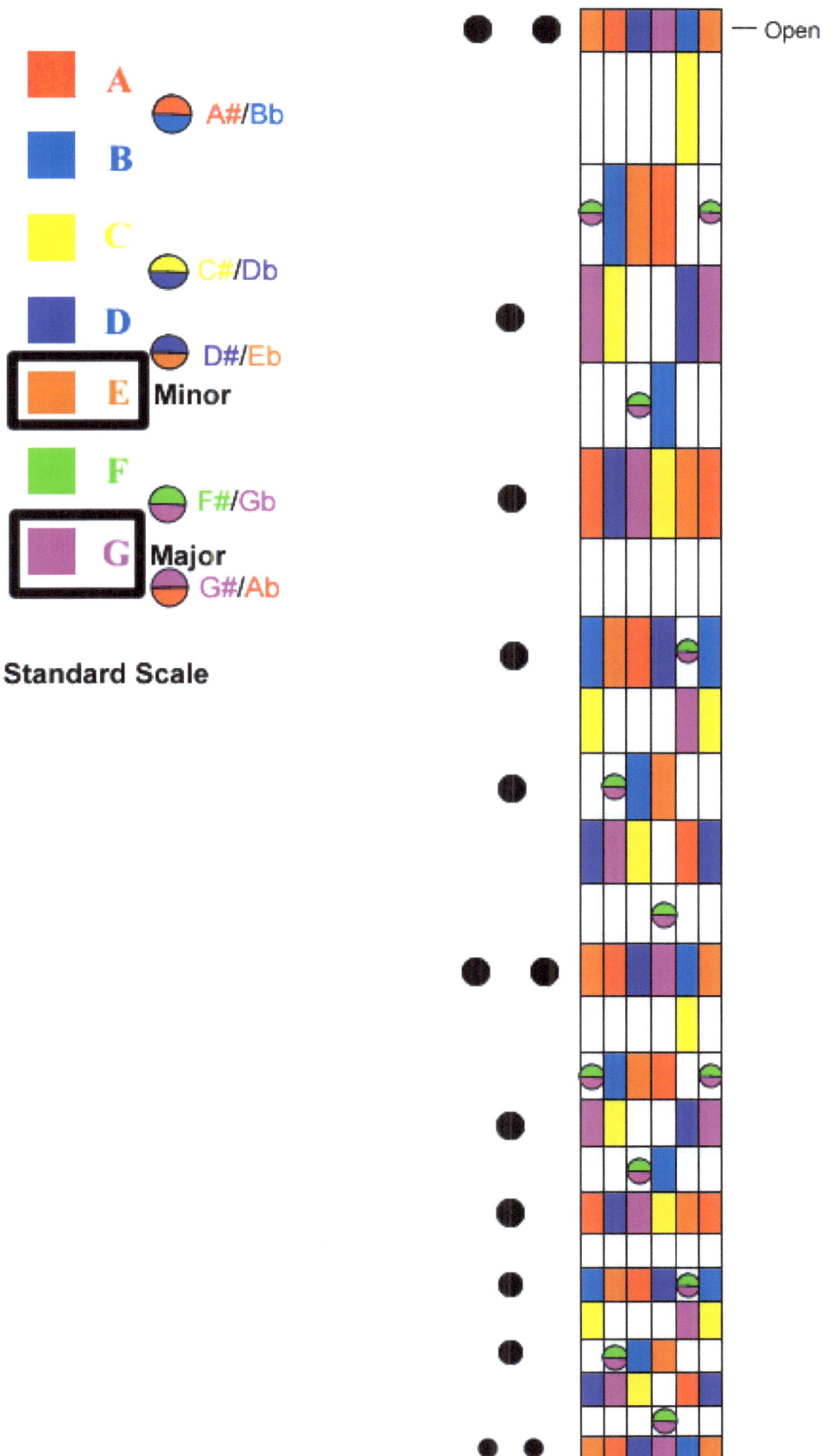

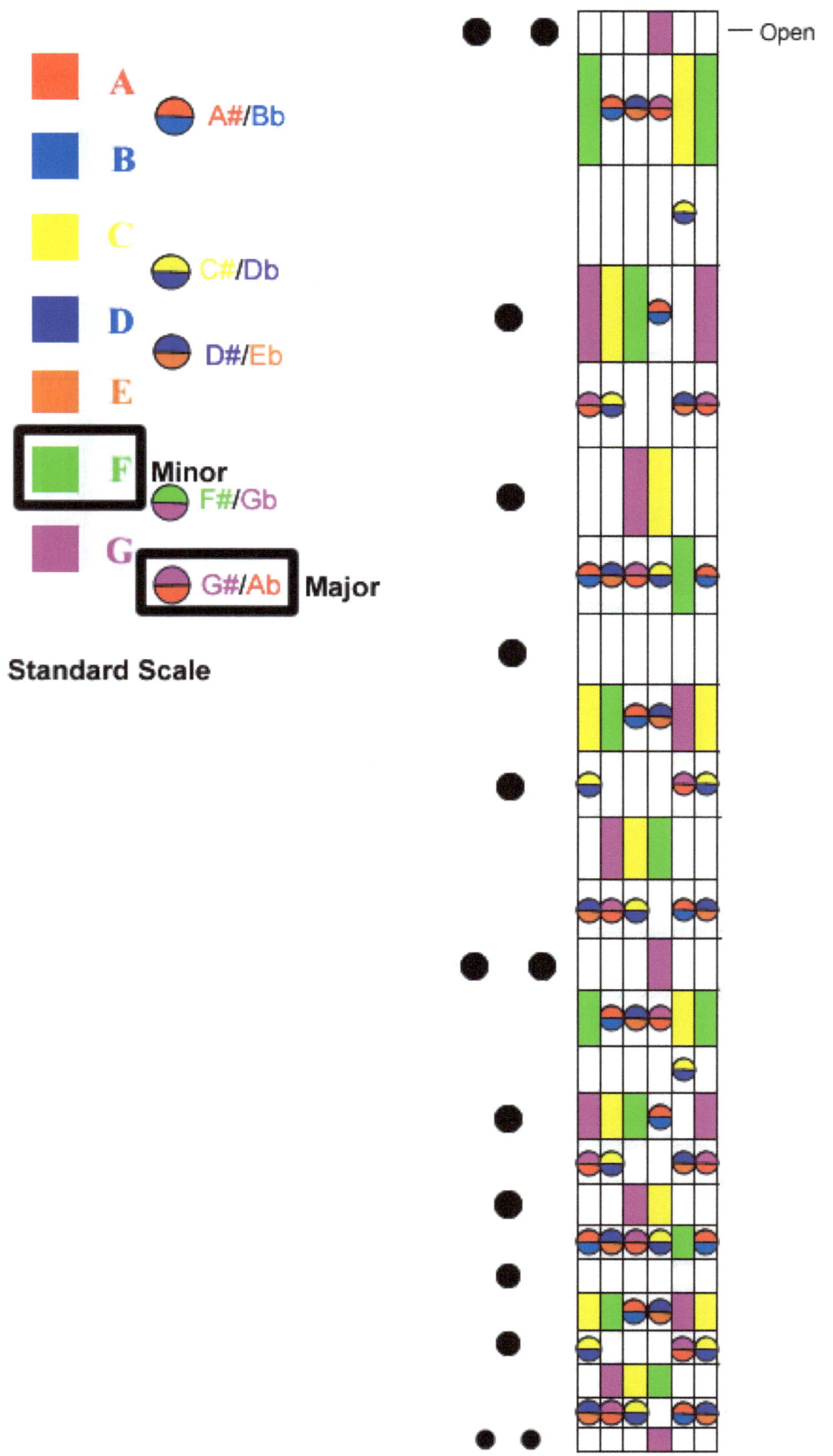

- Pentatonic Scale Box Patterns -

Major Pentatonic Scale Box Patterns

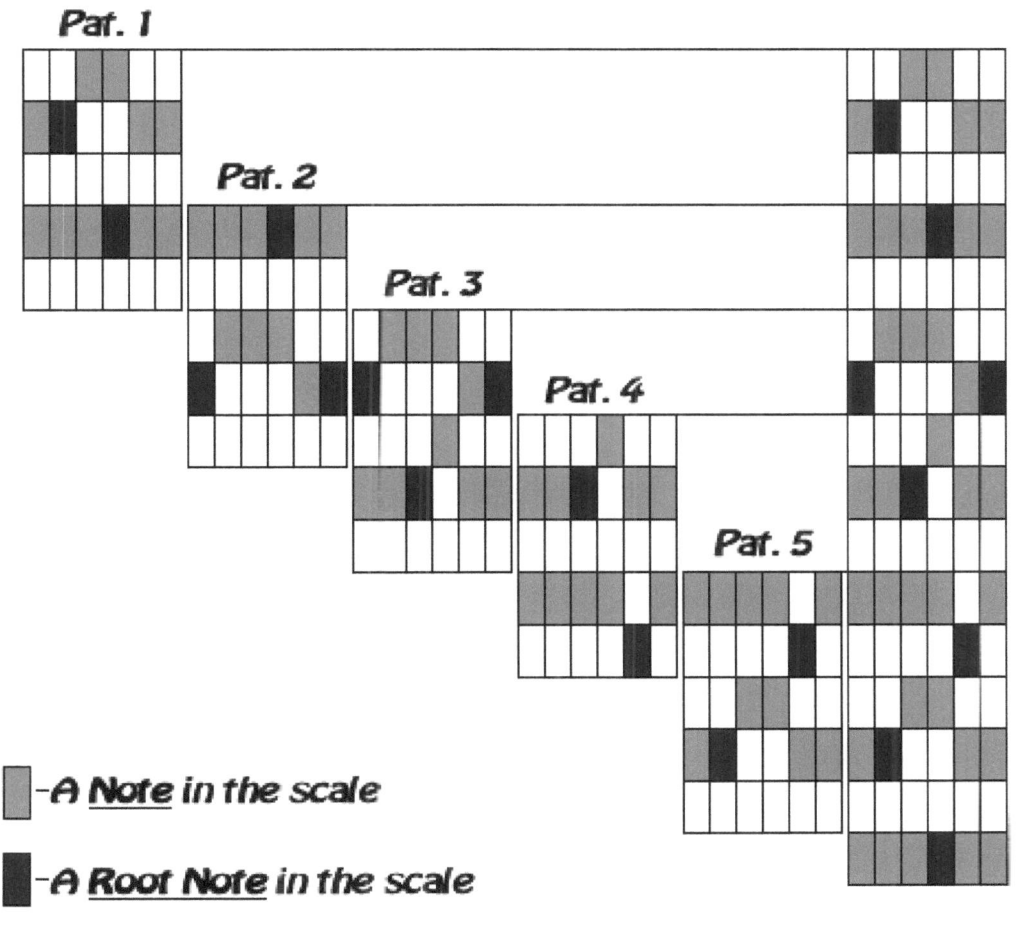

Minor Pentatonic Scale Box Patterns

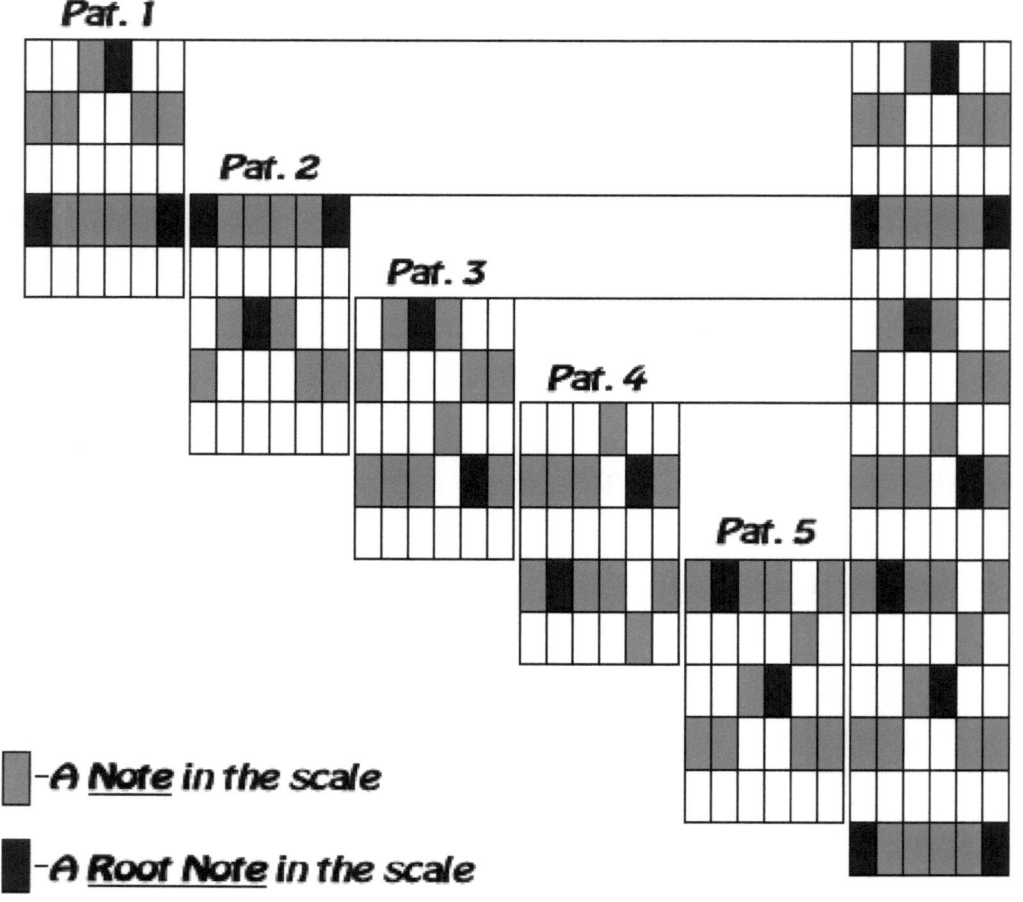

-Pentatonic Major/Minor Scales-

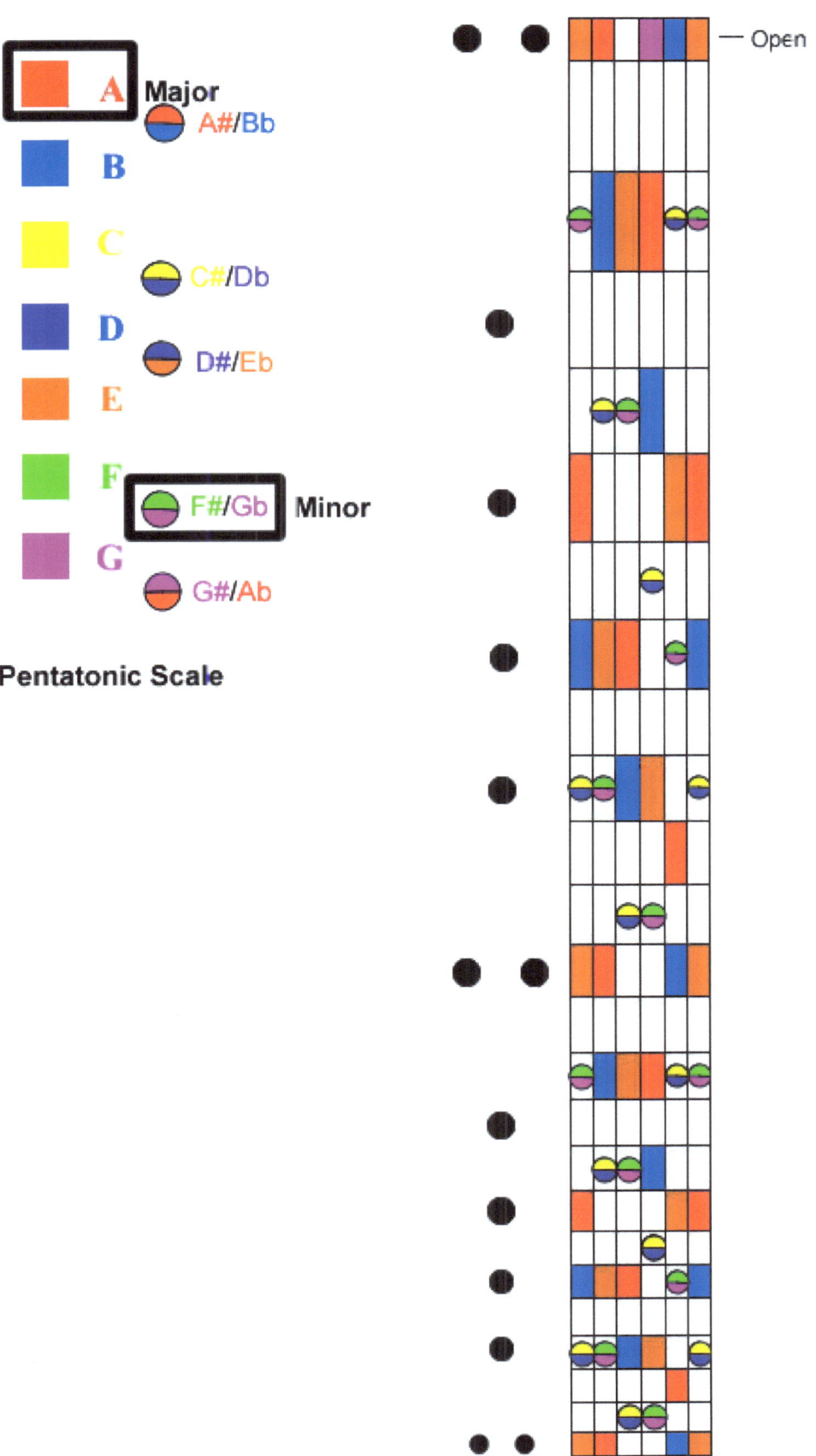

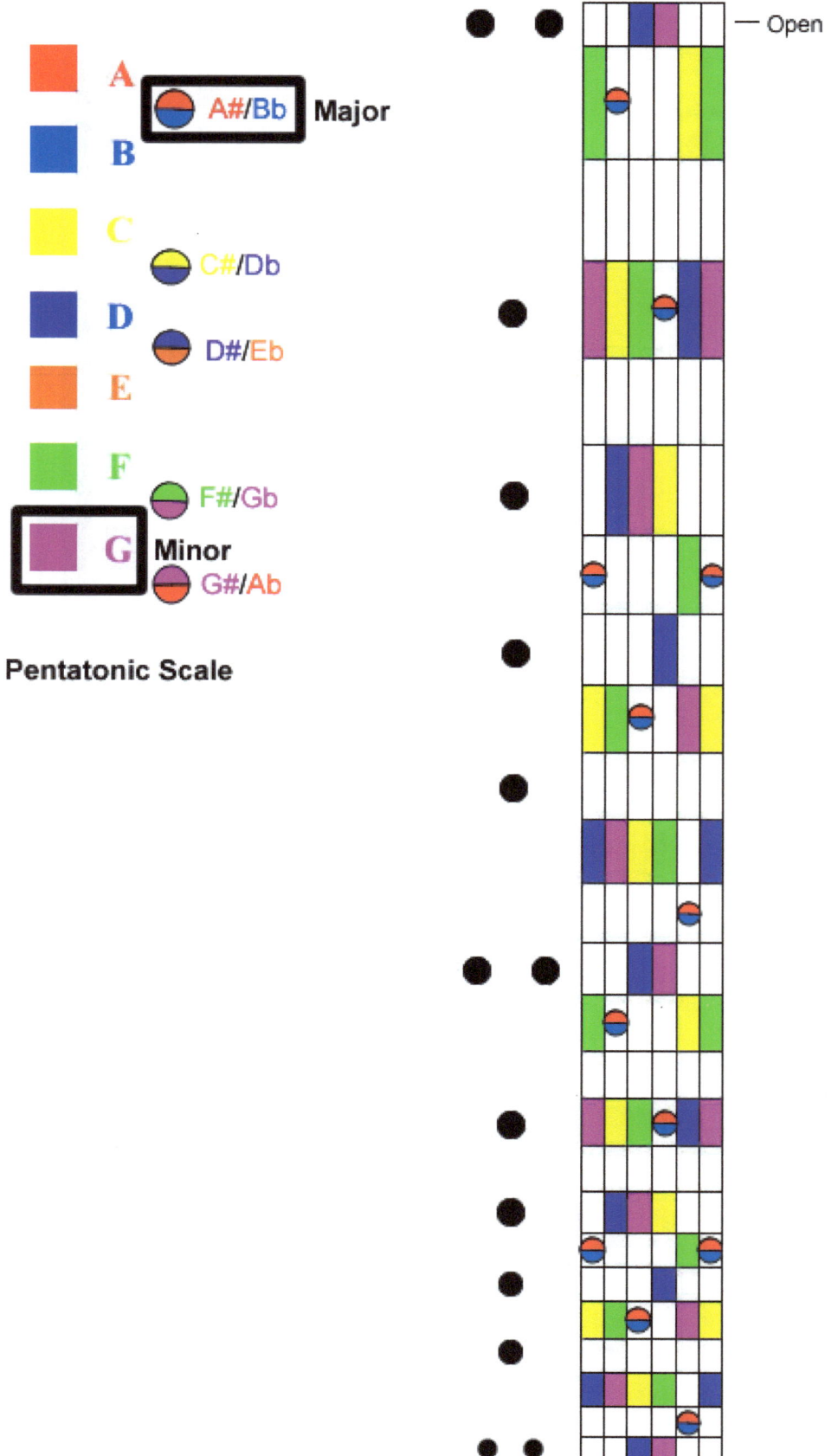

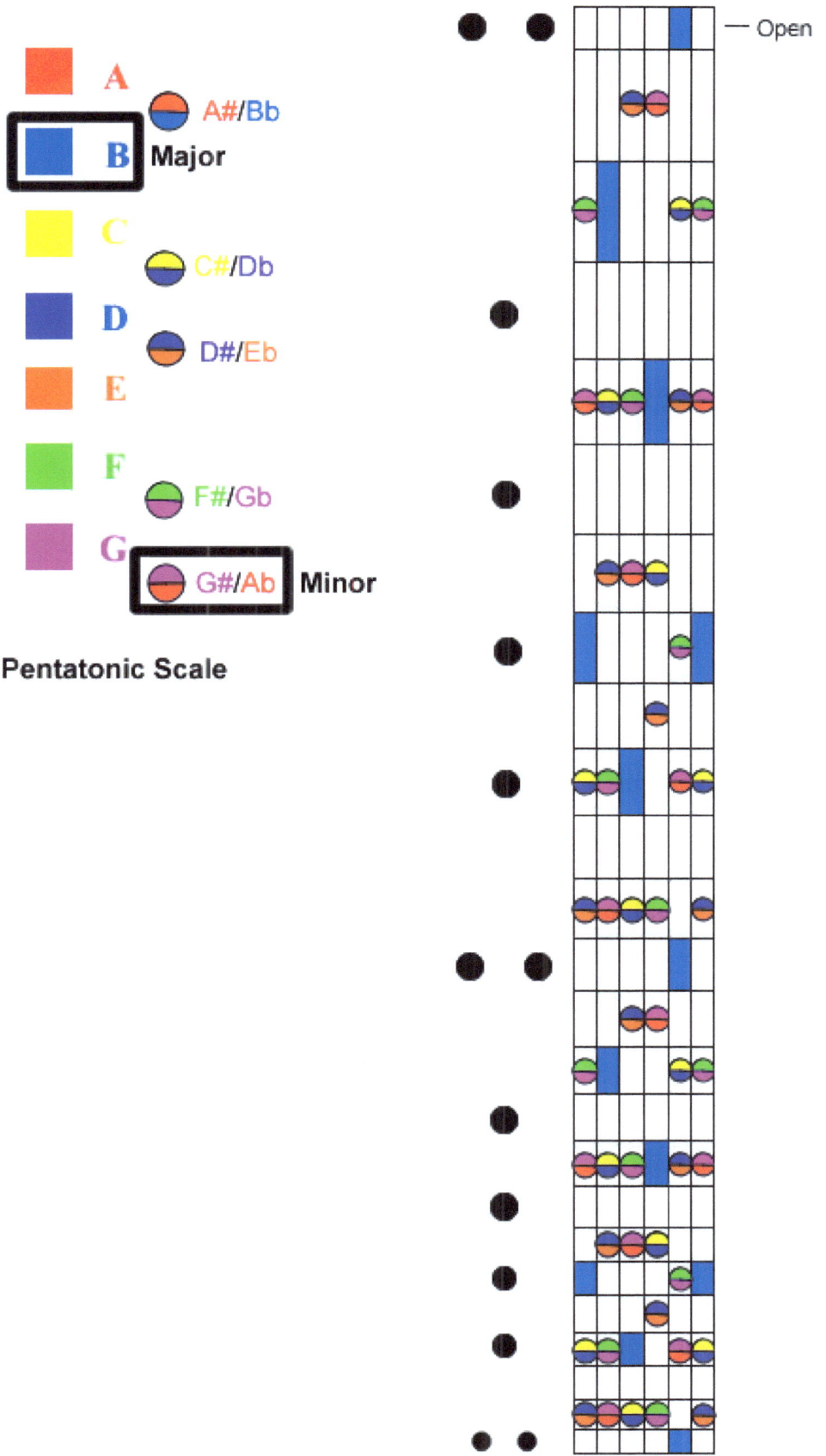

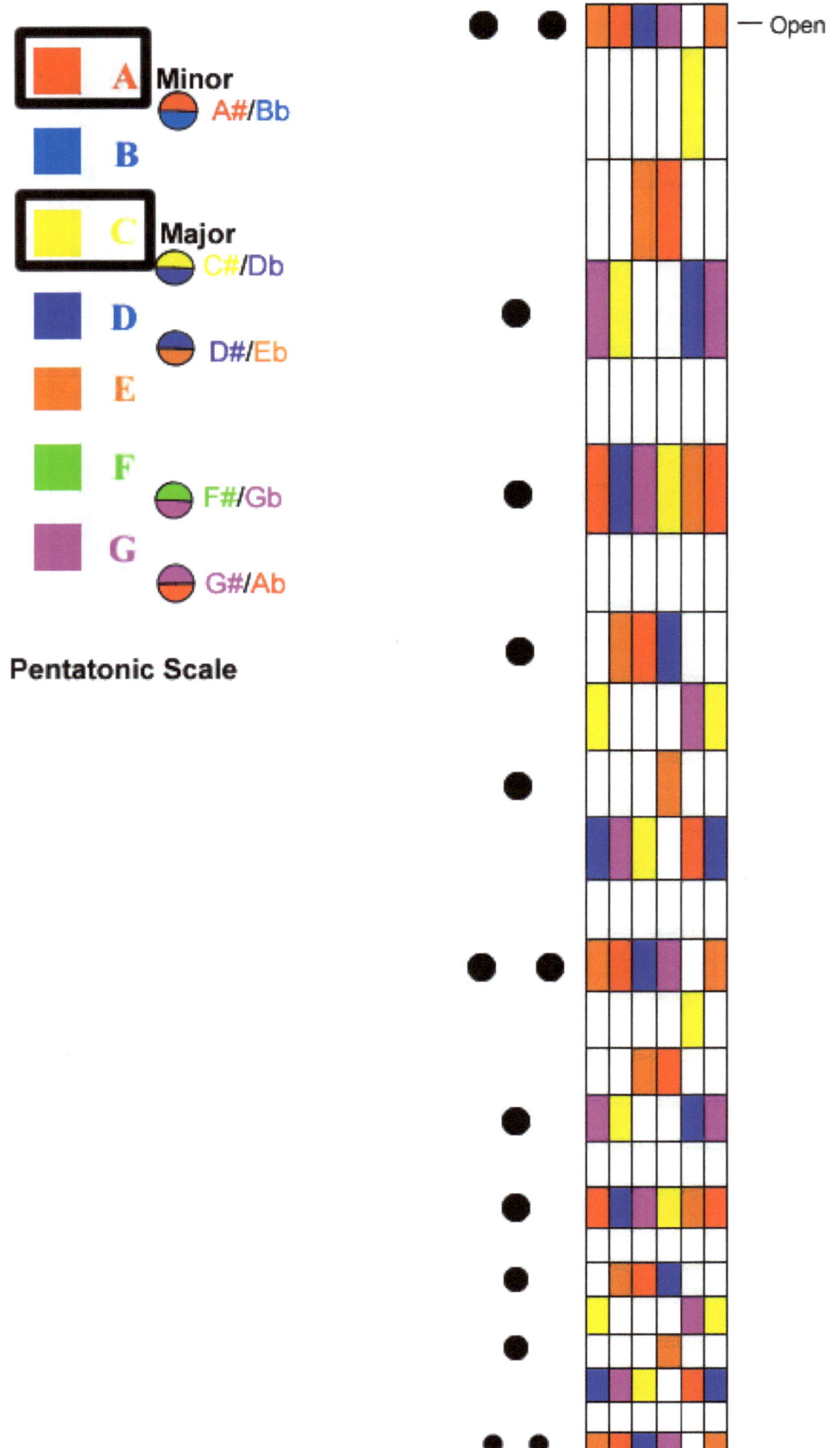

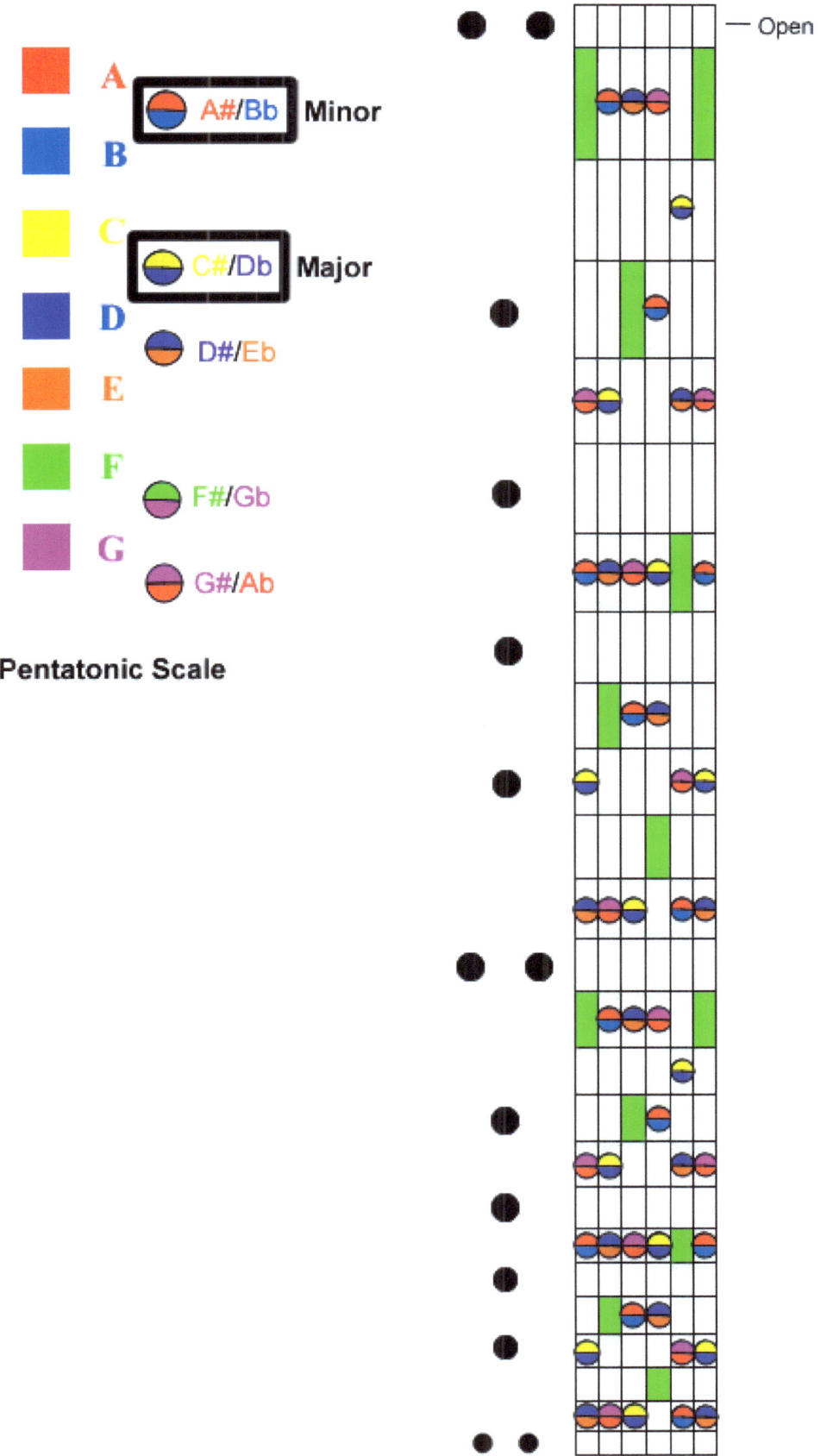

Pentatonic Scale

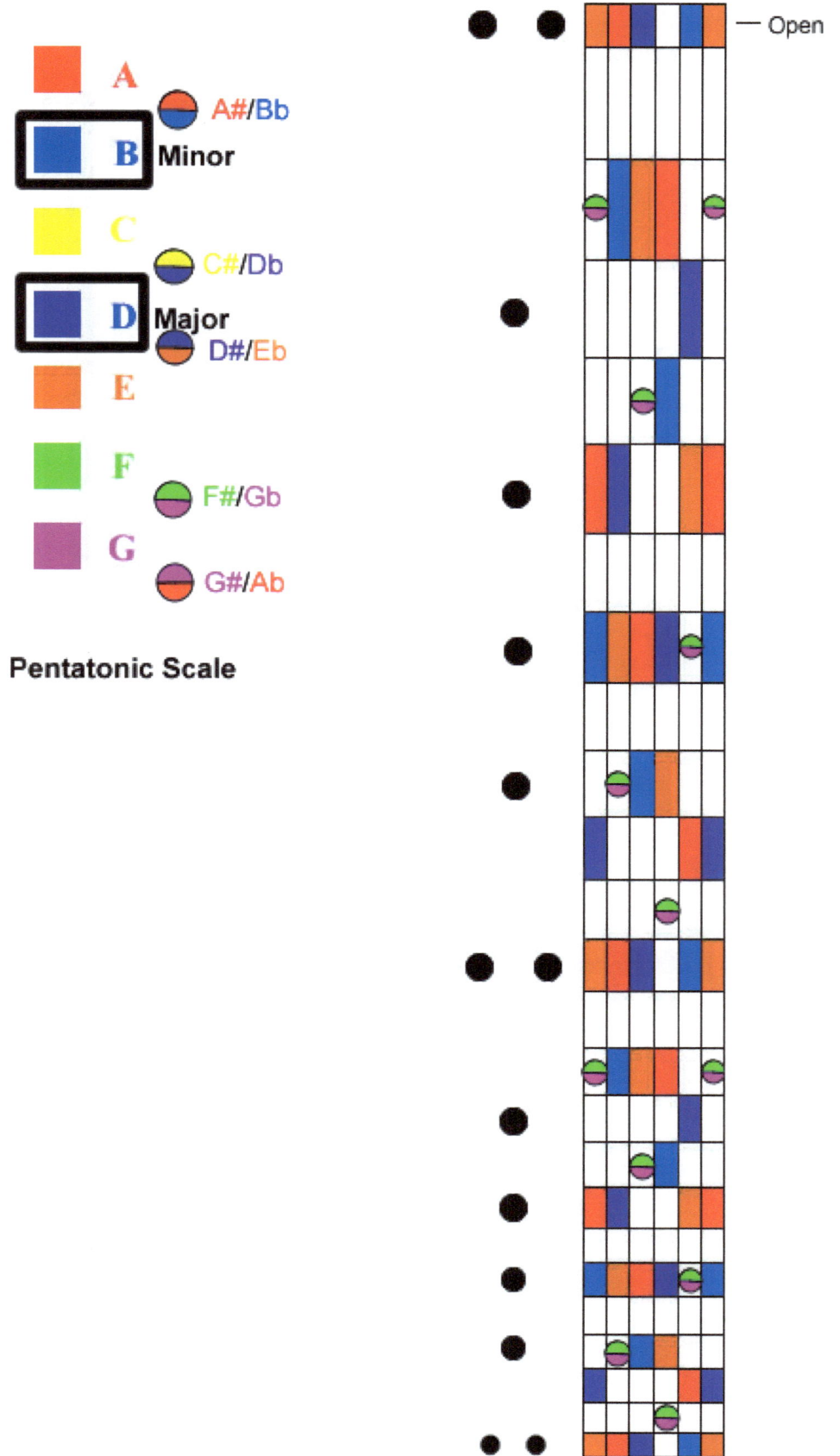

31

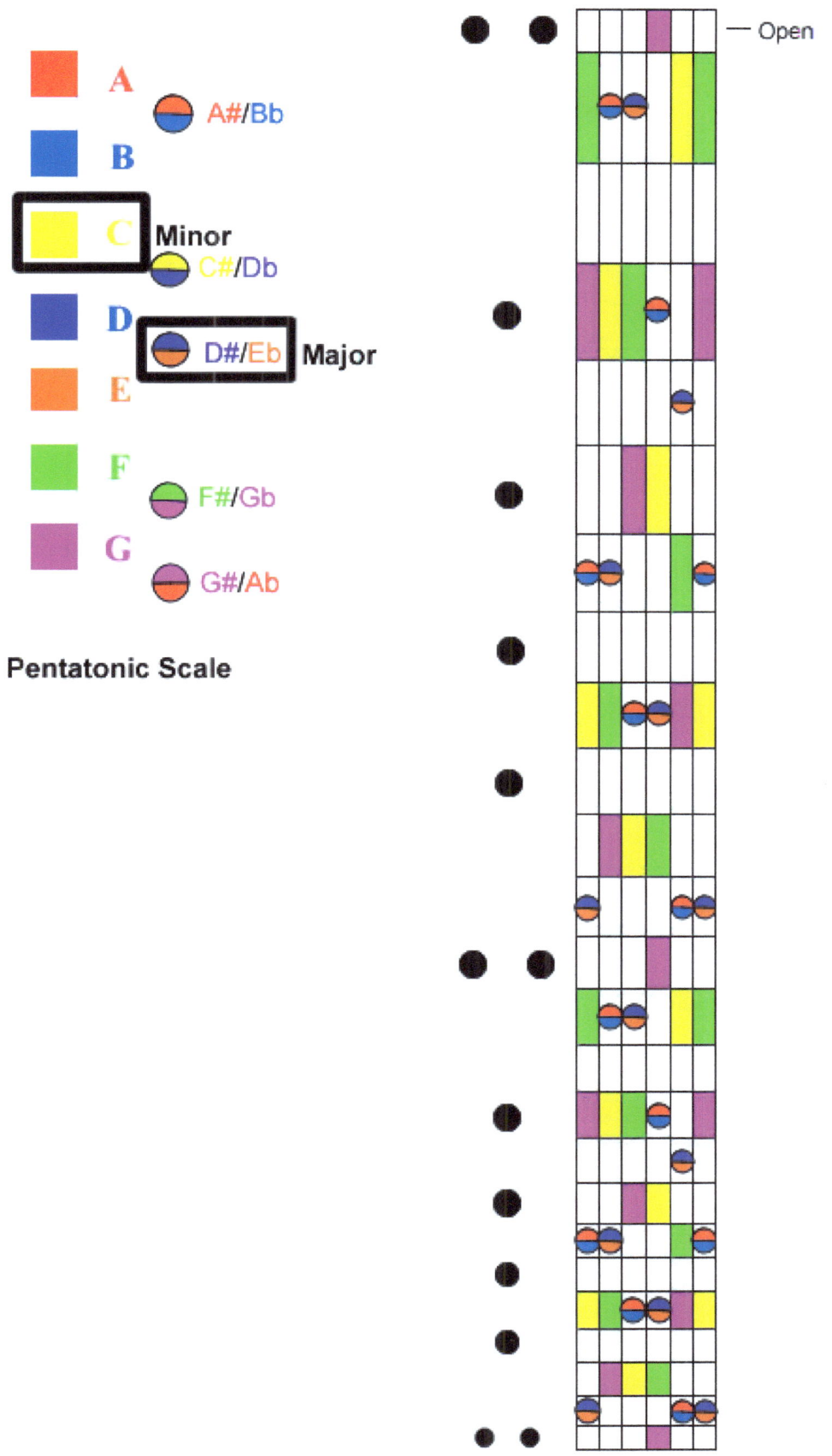

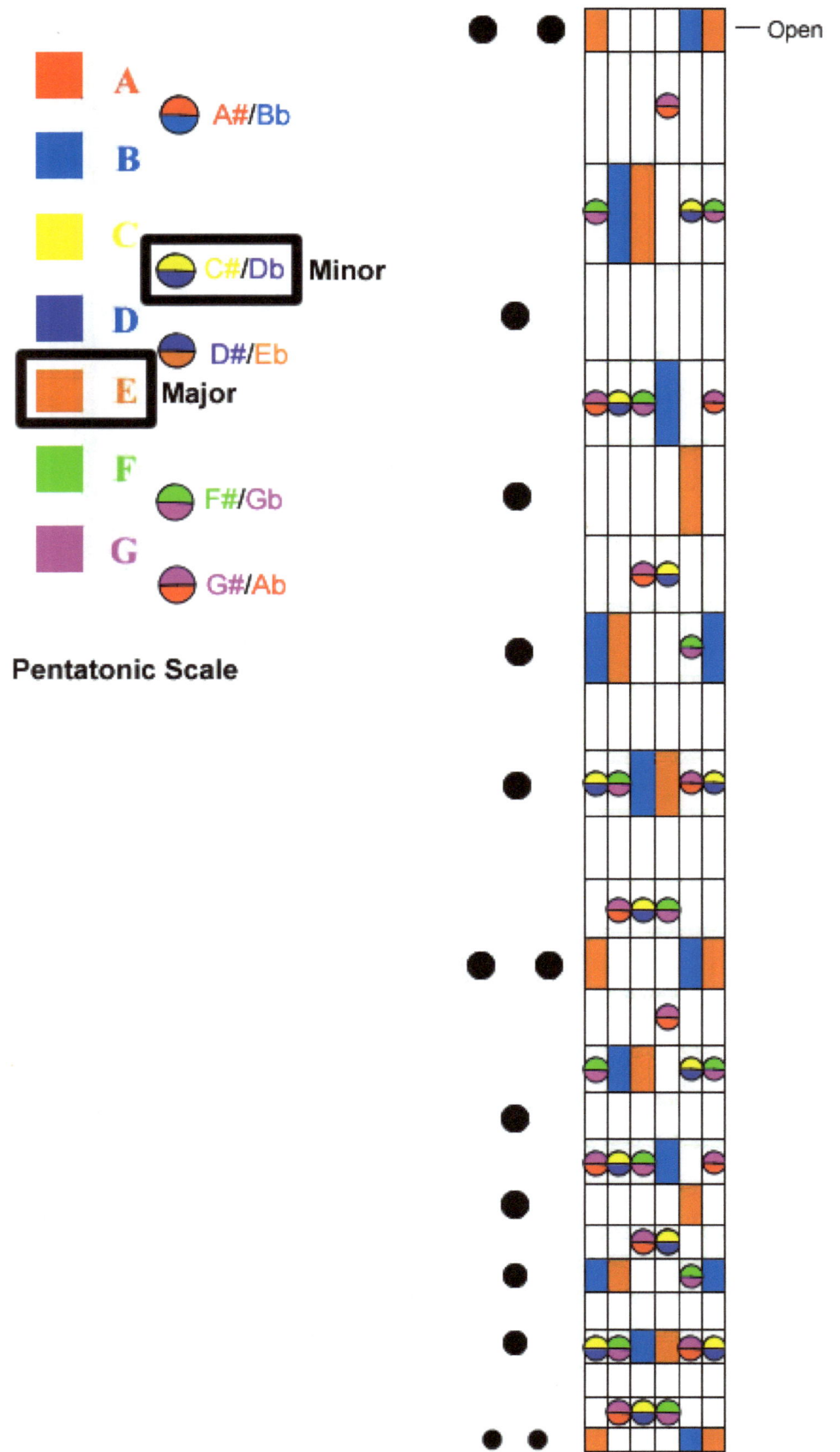

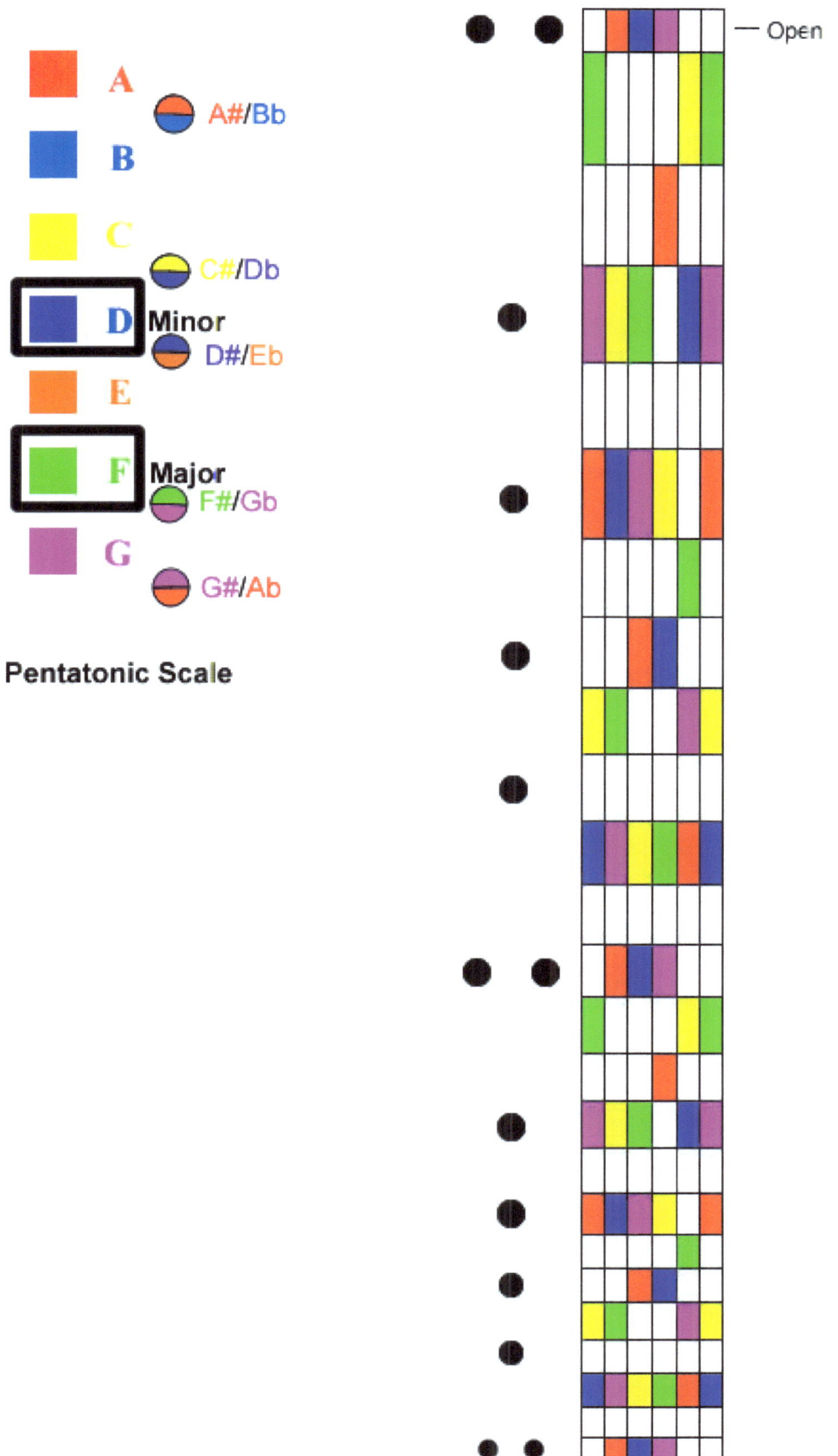

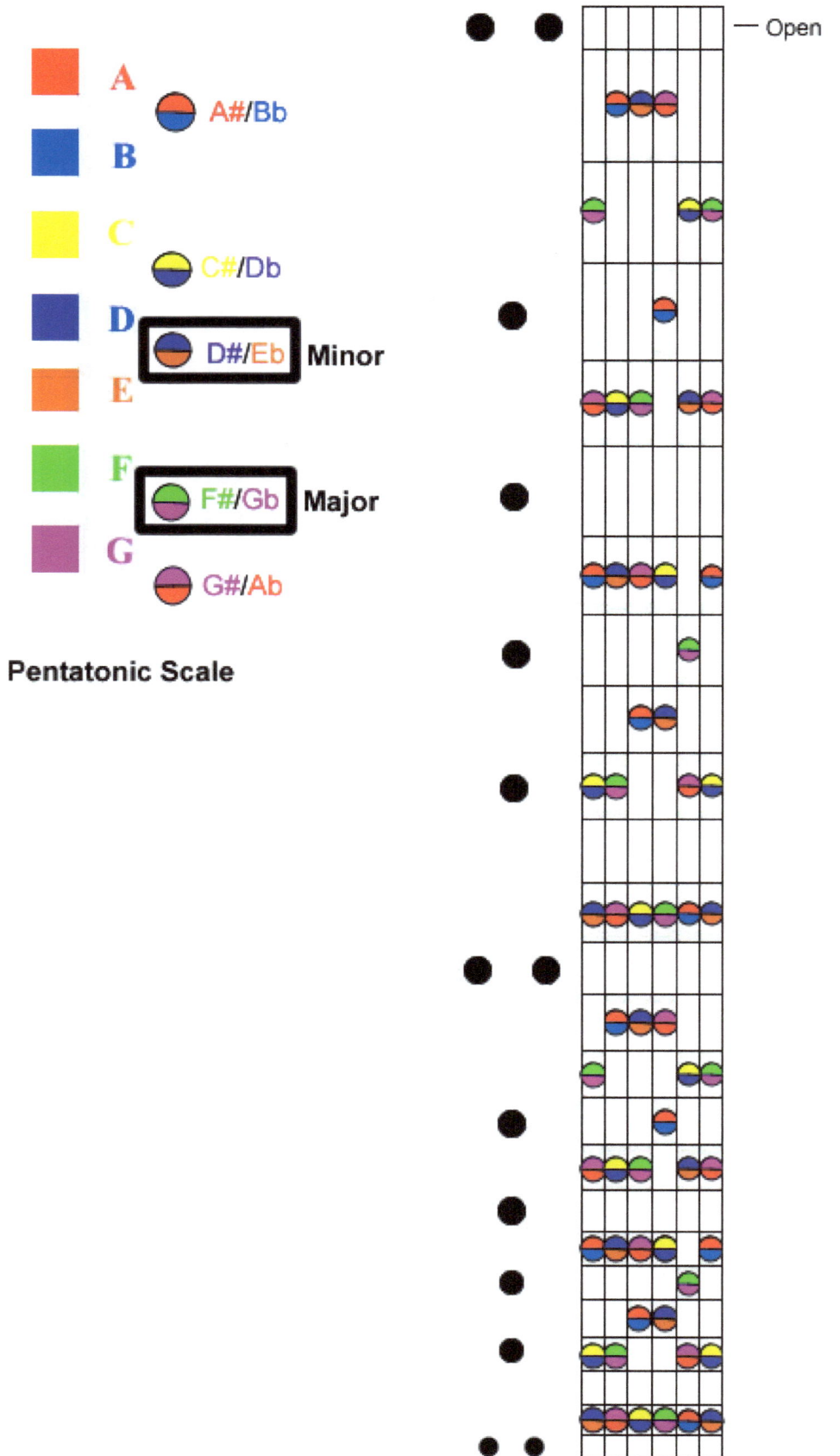

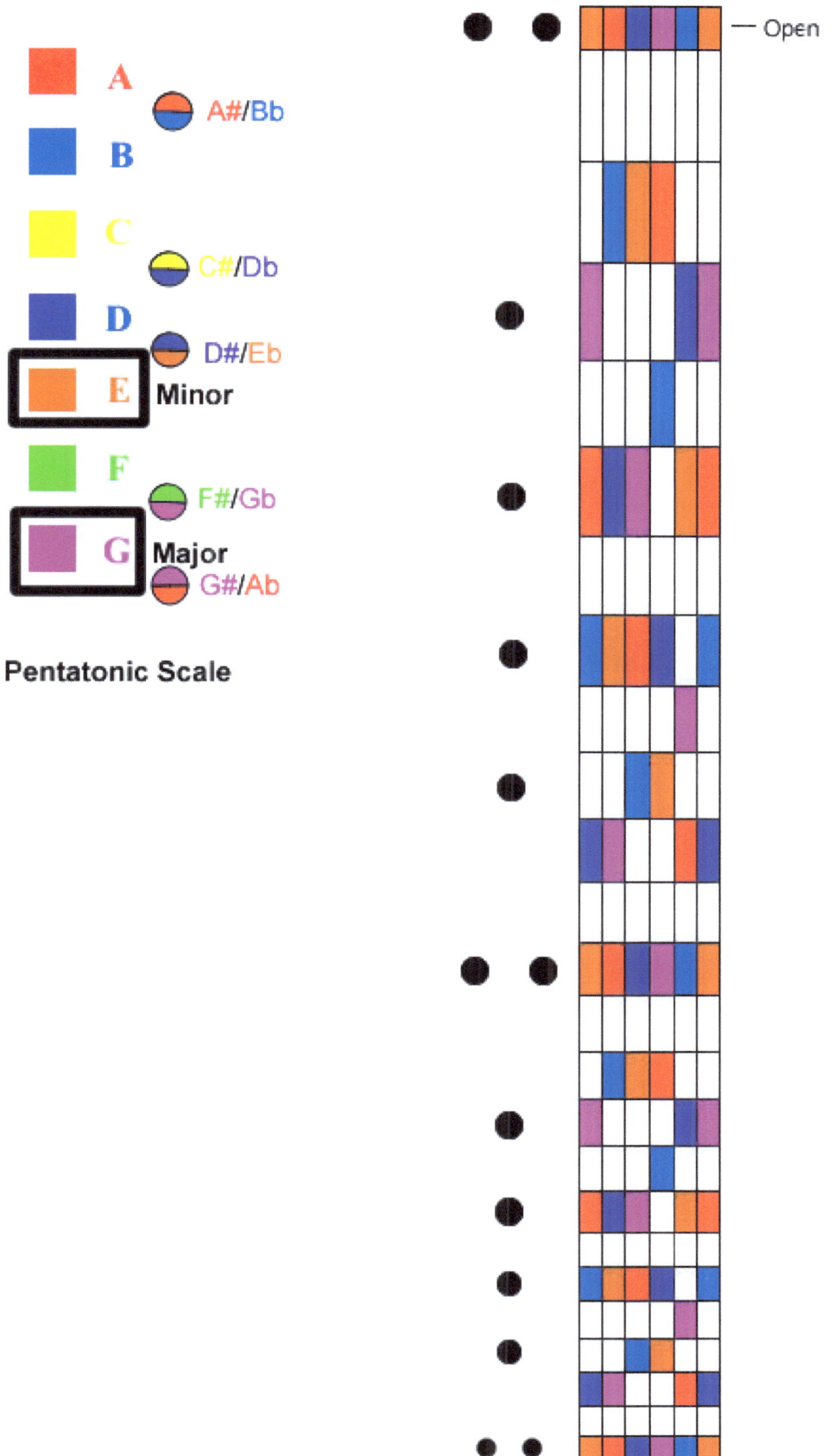

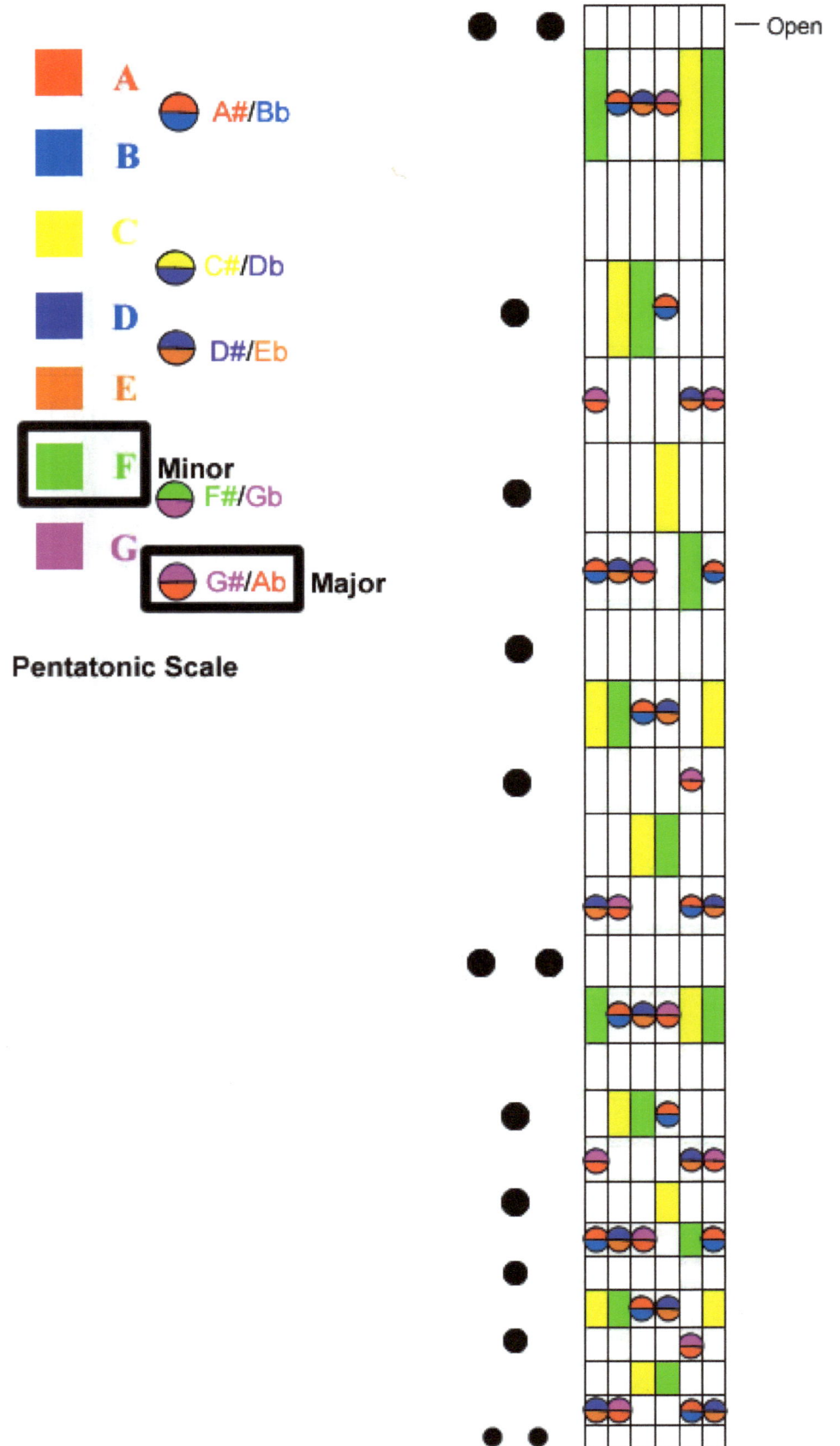

-Chords Introduction-

Chord Vocabulary: Major Chord

The Major chord takes its name from the Major Standard scale, using the first, third, and fifth degrees of that scale. The chord named C Major would therefore be named after the C Major Standard scale and include the notes, C, E, and G, also known as the first, third, and fifth degrees of the C Major Standard scale.

Chord Vocabulary: Minor Chord

The Minor chord takes its name from the Minor Standard scale, using the first, third, and fifth degrees of that scale. The chord named A Minor would therefore be named after the A Minor Standard scale and include the notes, A, C, and E, also known as the first, third, and fifth degrees of the A Minor Standard scale.

Chord Vocabulary: Dominant 7th Chord

The Dominant 7th chord, commonly known as "the 7th chord", uses the first, third, fifth, and flat seventh degrees of the Major Standard scale; flat seventh meaning the note a half step before the 7th degree of that scale. The chord named C7 would therefore include the notes, C, E, G, and Bb, also known as the first, third, fifth, and flat seventh degrees of the C Major Standard scale.

Chord Vocabulary: Major 7th Chord

The Major 7th chord takes its name from the Major Standard scale, using the first, third, fifth, and seventh degrees of that scale. The chord named C Major 7 would therefore be named after the C Major Standard scale and include the notes, C, E, G, and B also known as the first, third, fifth, and seventh degrees of the C Major Standard scale.

Chord Vocabulary: Minor 7th Chord

The Minor 7th chord takes its name from the Minor Standard scale, using the first, third, fifth and seventh degrees of that scale. The chord named A Minor would therefore be named after the A Minor Standard scale and include the notes, A, C, E, and G also known as the first, third, fifth, and seventh degrees of the A Minor Standard scale.

Chord Vocabulary: Movable Chord Shapes

A chord shape is a grouping of notes on the grid of the fretboard that represents the notes included in a particular chord type. The five chord types just previously defined as, Major Chord, Minor Chord, Dominant 7th Chord, Major 7th Chord, and Minor 7th Chord, each have their own specific chord shape or grouping of notes that when played together create the sound of that particular chord.

<u>Key Concept:</u> Movable Chord Shapes are used very much the same way for memorizing chord types as box patterns are used to quickly memorize a particular scale type. The notes on the guitar fretboard are organized and designed in such a way that once a particular chord shape is known in one key, it is known in every key, by simply aligning the root note of the movable chord shape to the desired key.

What makes each of these chord shapes movable is a technique called barring.

When a chord shape is played at the very top of the fretboard, or in open position, so that some strings ring out without a finger placed on them, the slotted piece of material which holds the strings in place, called the nut, acts as the barre for all open chords.

Barring a chord is how you recreate the open position movable chord shapes further up the guitar fretboard by using your index finger placed across the width of the guitar neck to recreate the nut at the top of the fretboard, so that each chord is framed by your barring index finger the way that same chord shape is framed by the nut in open position.

Each chord as with each scale, is defined by their root note. The movable chord shapes get their root note from either the E string or the A string as defined by each particular chord type. When a movable chord shape is played in the open position, the open E or A string in that particular chord type will be the root but as you move your index finger into position to play the chord shape in a barred position the root note will now be in the position fretted by that index finger.

While there is a movable chord shape for all five types of chords included in this book, other common, traditional, non-movable variations are also included for reference.

-Movable Chord Shapes-

E String Root Major Chord Movable Chord Shape

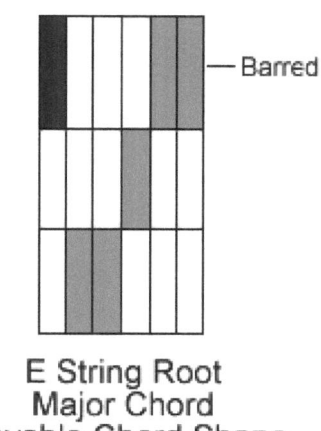

E String Root
Major Chord
Movable Chord Shape

▓ -A **_Note_** in the chord

■ -A **_Root Note_** in the chord

E String Root Minor Chord Movable Chord Shape

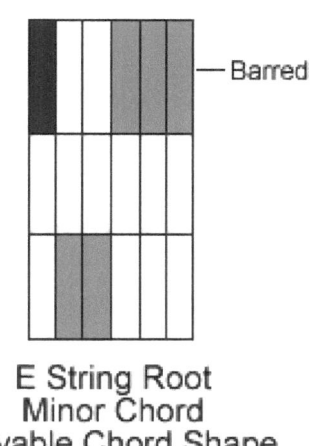

E String Root
Minor Chord
Movable Chord Shape

▓ -A **_Note_** in the chord

■ -A **_Root Note_** in the chord

E String Root Dominant 7th Chord Movable Chord Shape

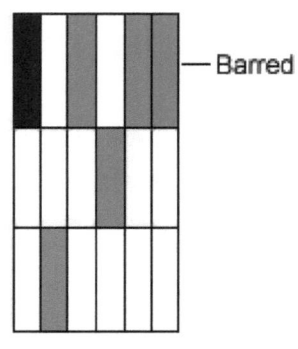

E String Root
Dominant 7th Chord
Movable Chord Shape

■ -A **_Note_** in the chord

■ -A **_Root Note_** in the chord

A String Root Major Chord Movable Chord Shape

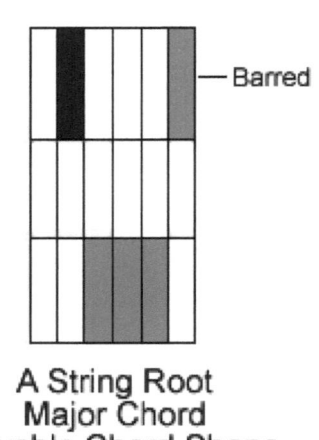

A String Root
Major Chord
Movable Chord Shape

■ -A **_Note_** in the chord

■ -A **_Root Note_** in the chord

A String Root Minor Chord Movable Chord Shape

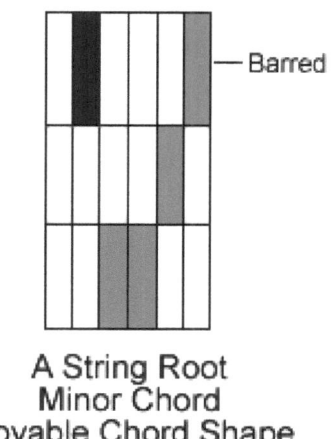

A String Root
Minor Chord
Movable Chord Shape

▪ — Barred

▫ - A **Note** in the chord

▪ - A **Root Note** in the chord

A String Root Dominant 7th Chord Movable Chord Shape

A String Root
Dominant 7th Chord
Movable Chord Shape

— Barred

▫ - A **Note** in the chord

▪ - A **Root Note** in the chord

A String Root Major 7th Chord Movable Chord Shape

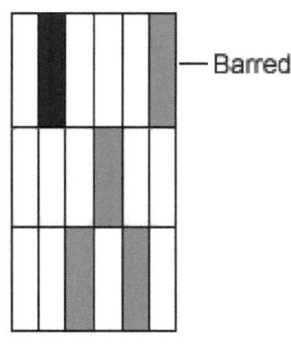

A String Root
Major 7th Chord
Movable Chord Shape

■ – A **_Note_** in the chord

■ – A **_Root Note_** in the chord

A String Root Minor 7th Chord Movable Chord Shape

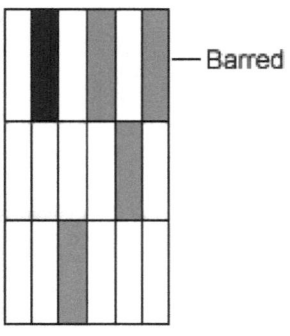

A String Root
Minor 7th Chord
Movable Chord Shape

■ – A **_Note_** in the chord

■ – A **_Root Note_** in the chord

-Major Chords-

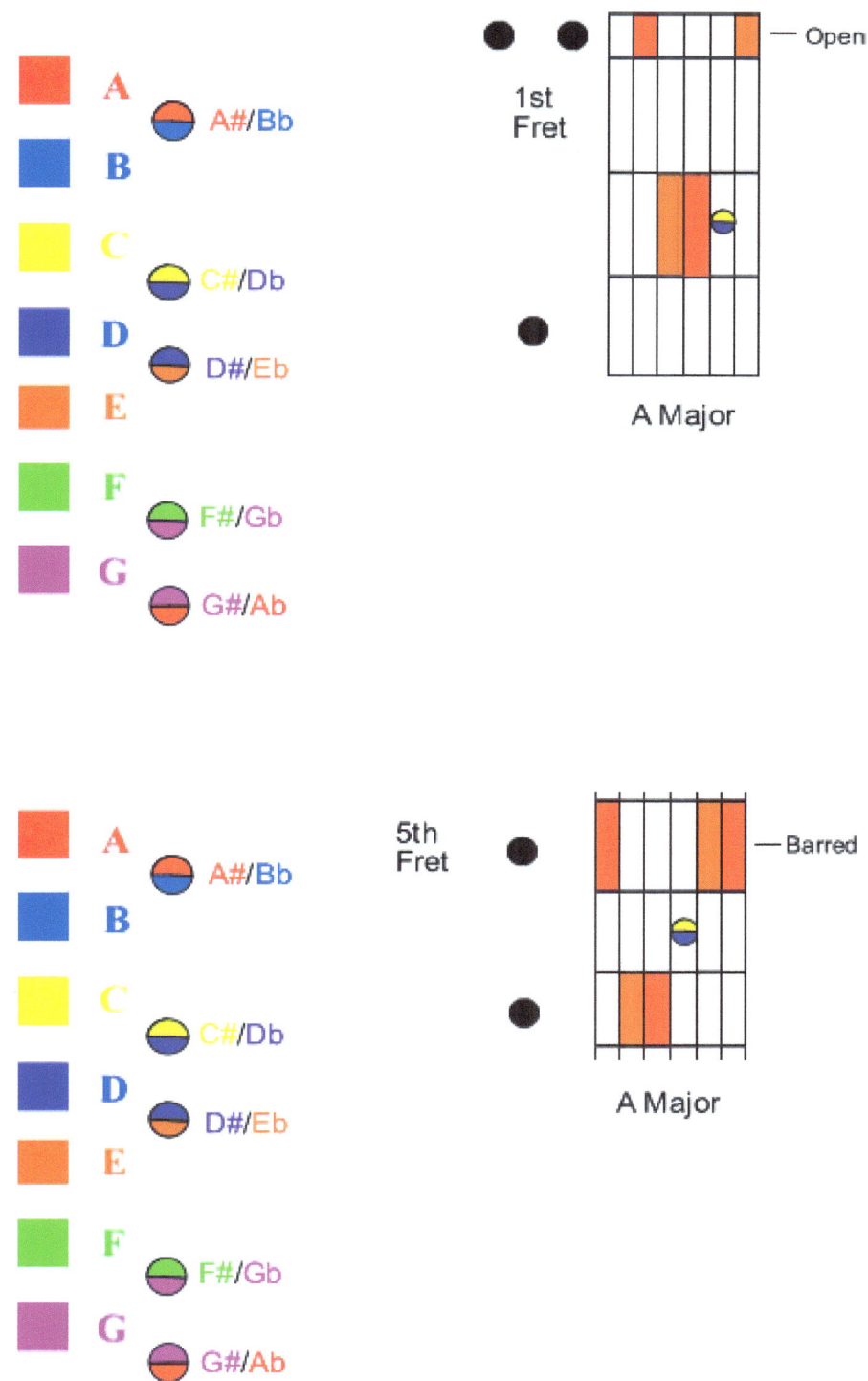

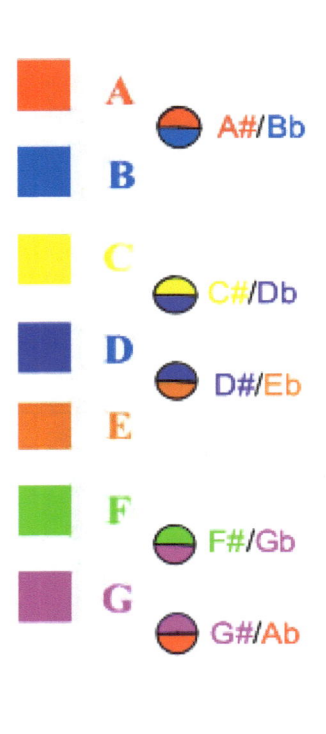
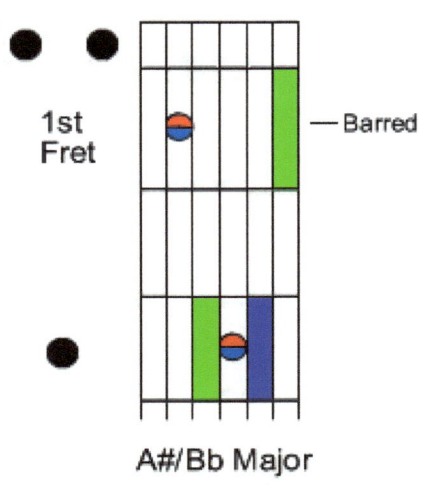

A#/Bb Major

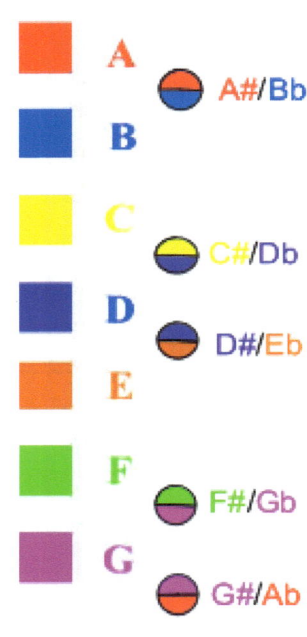
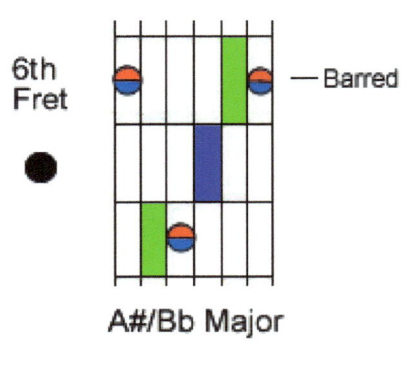

A#/Bb Major

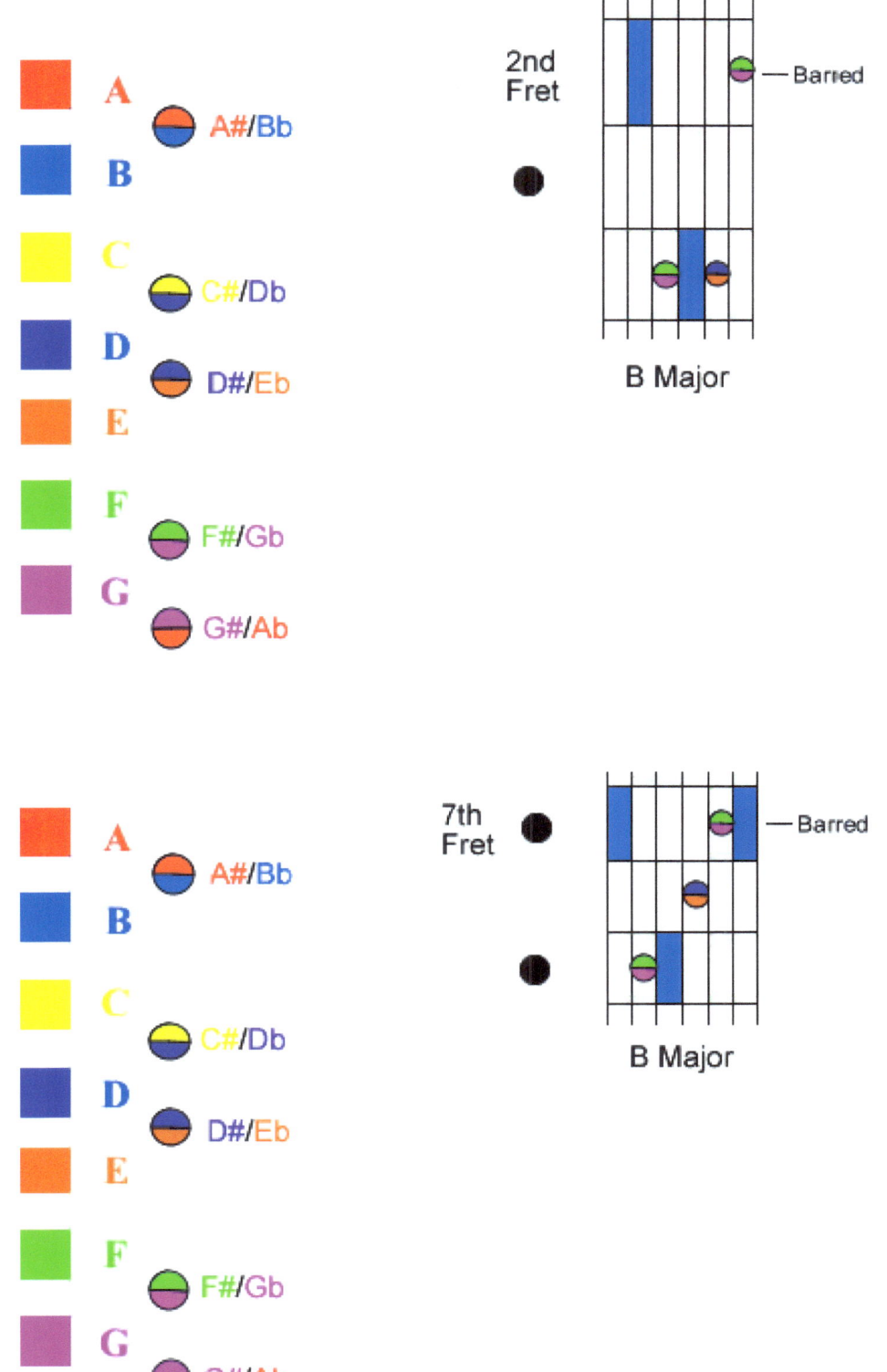

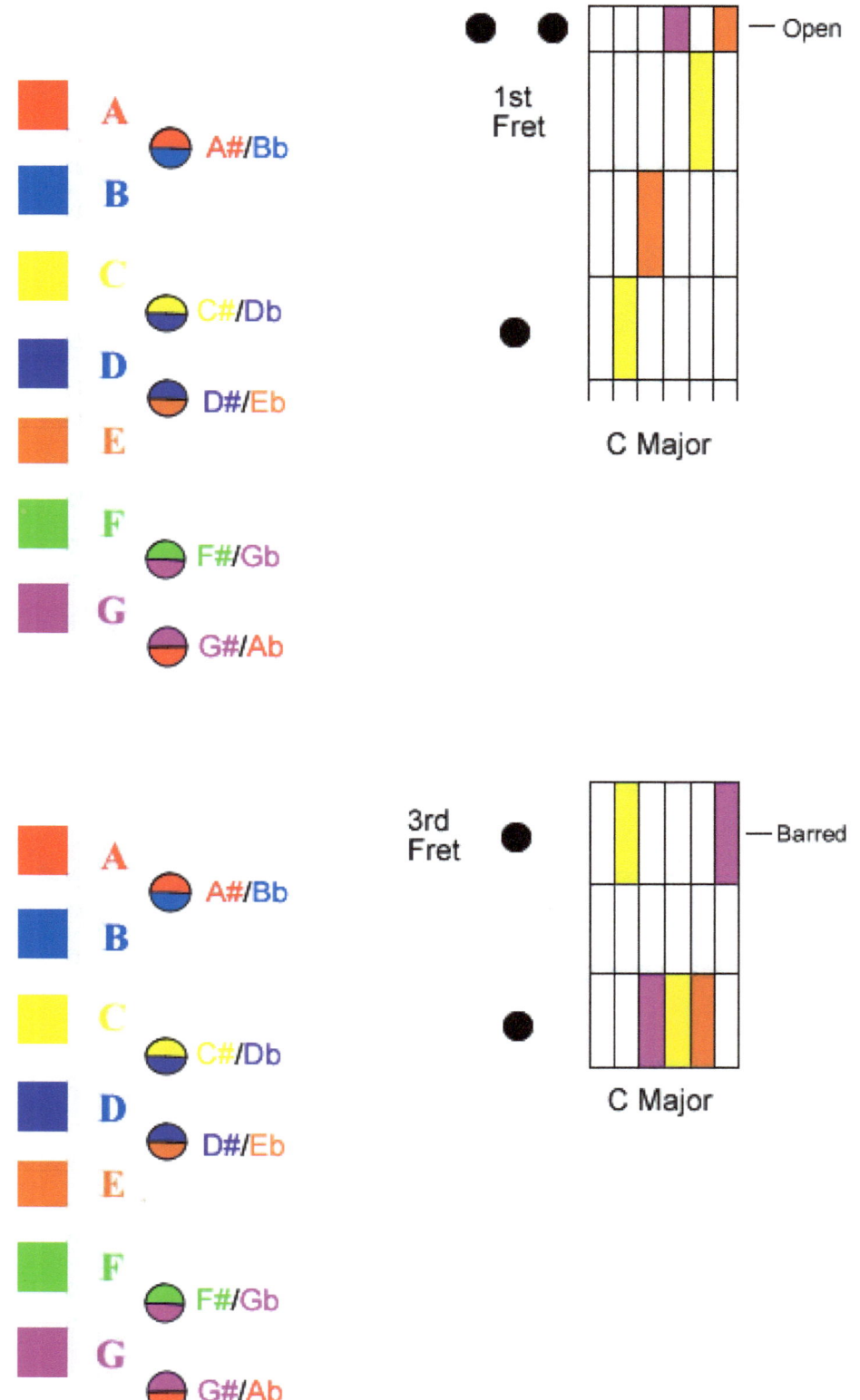

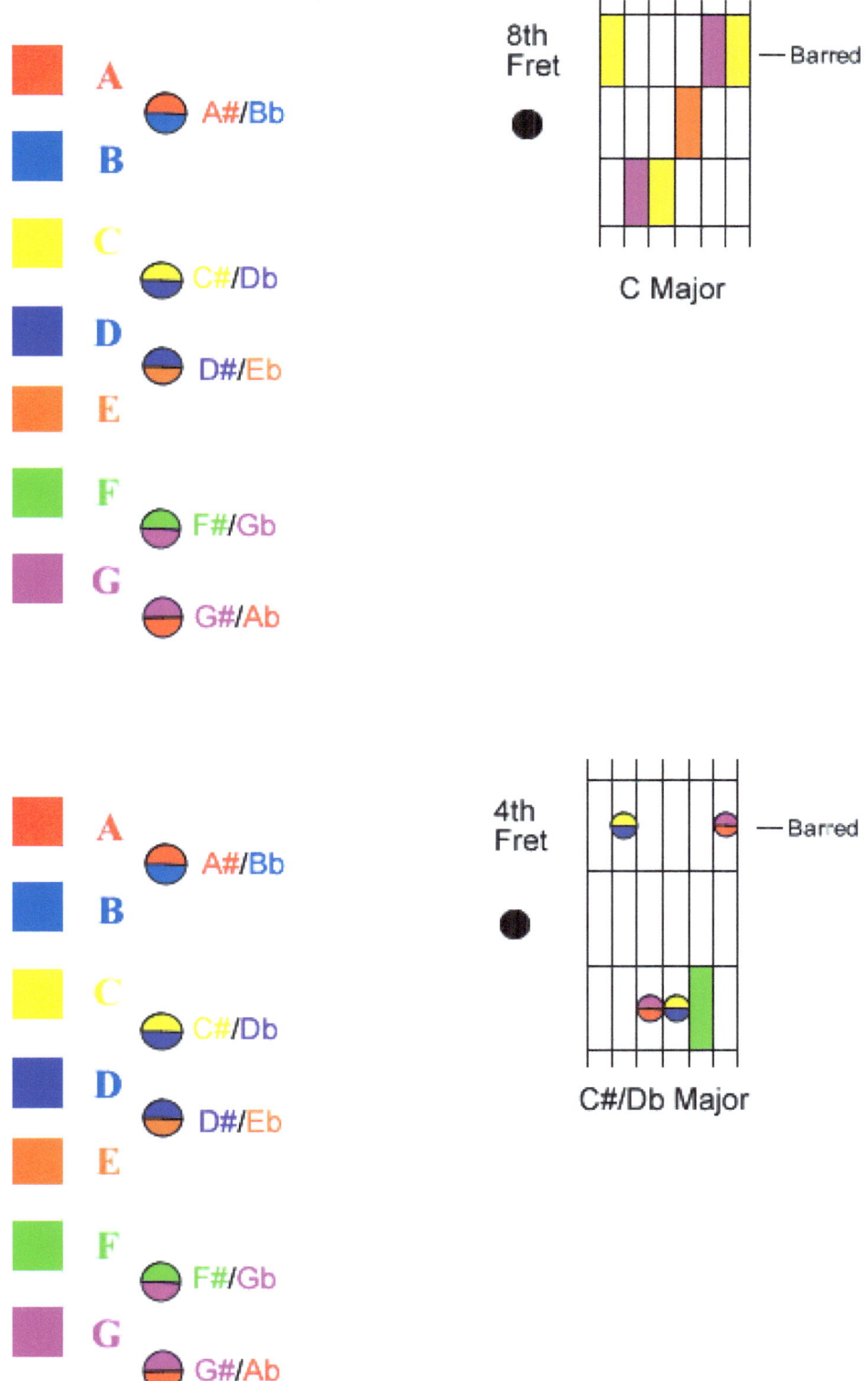

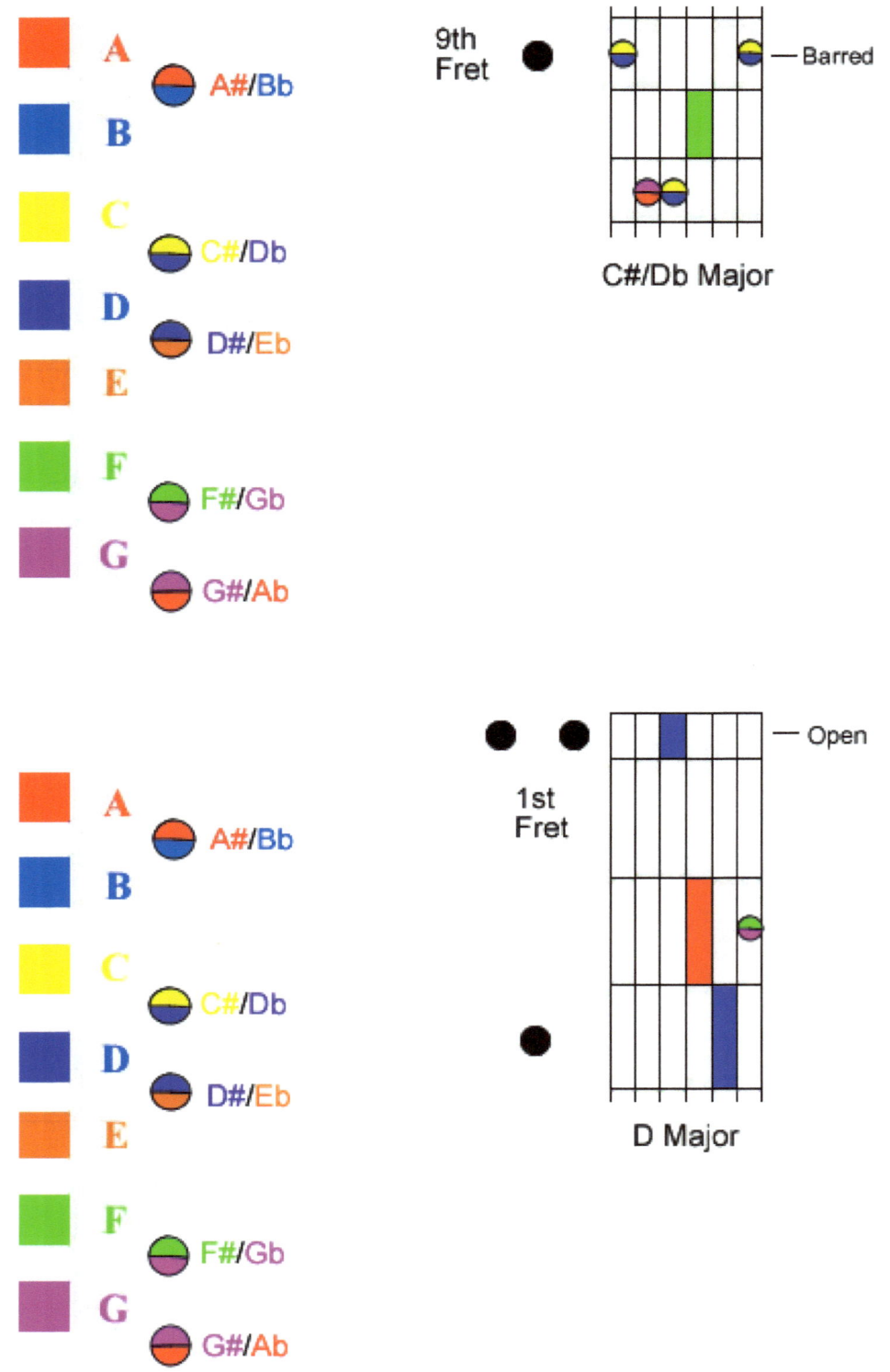

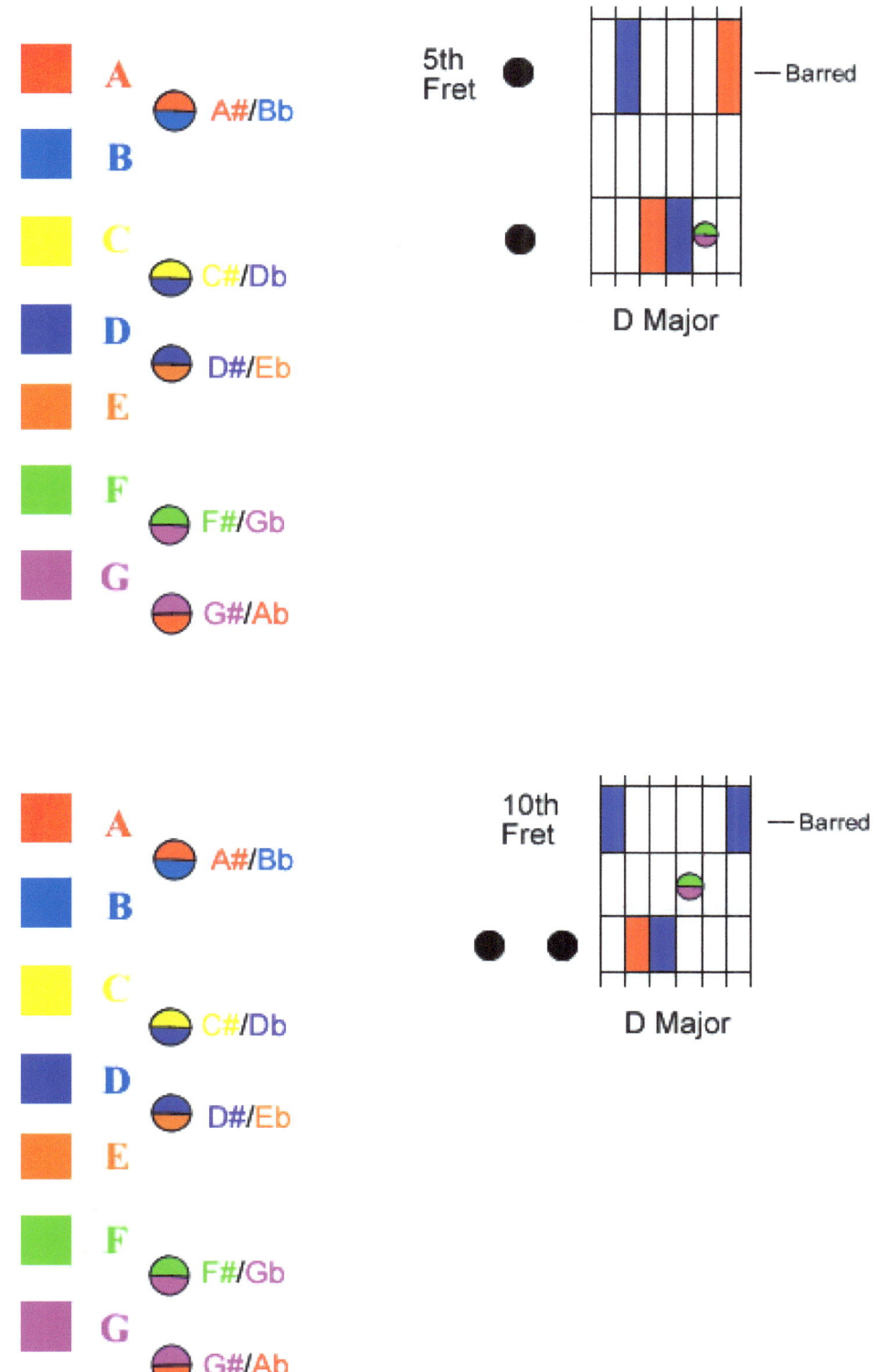

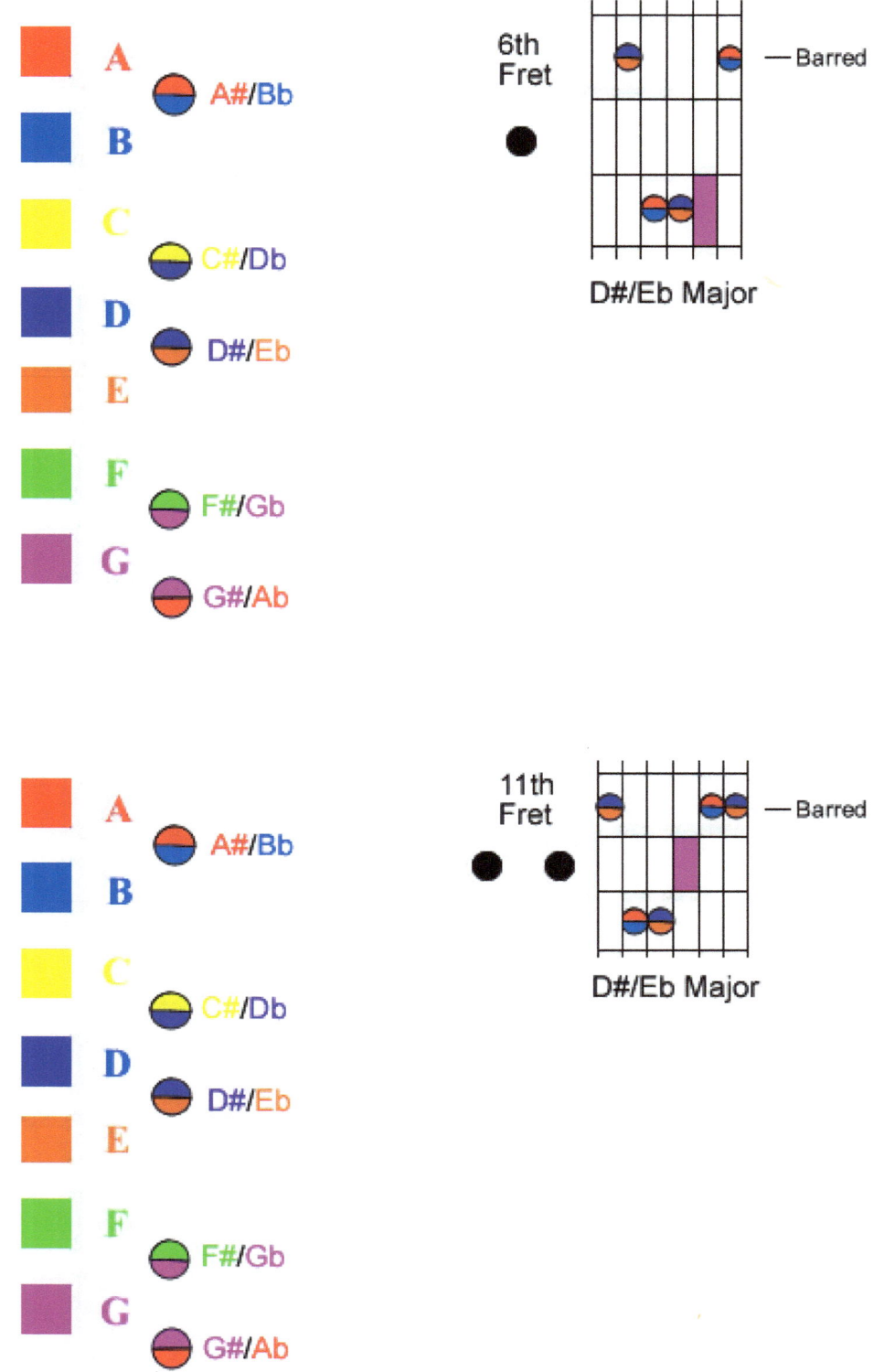

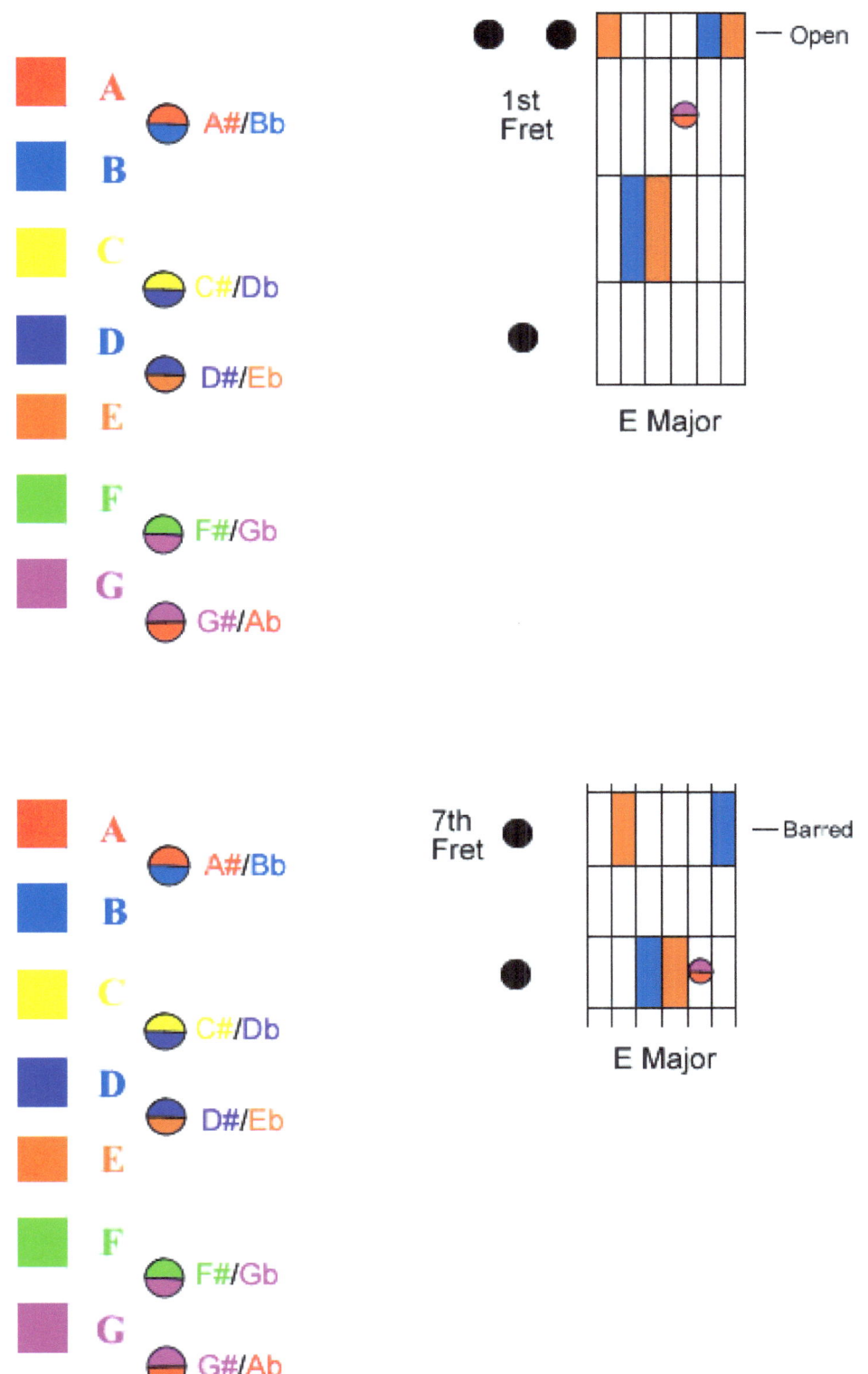

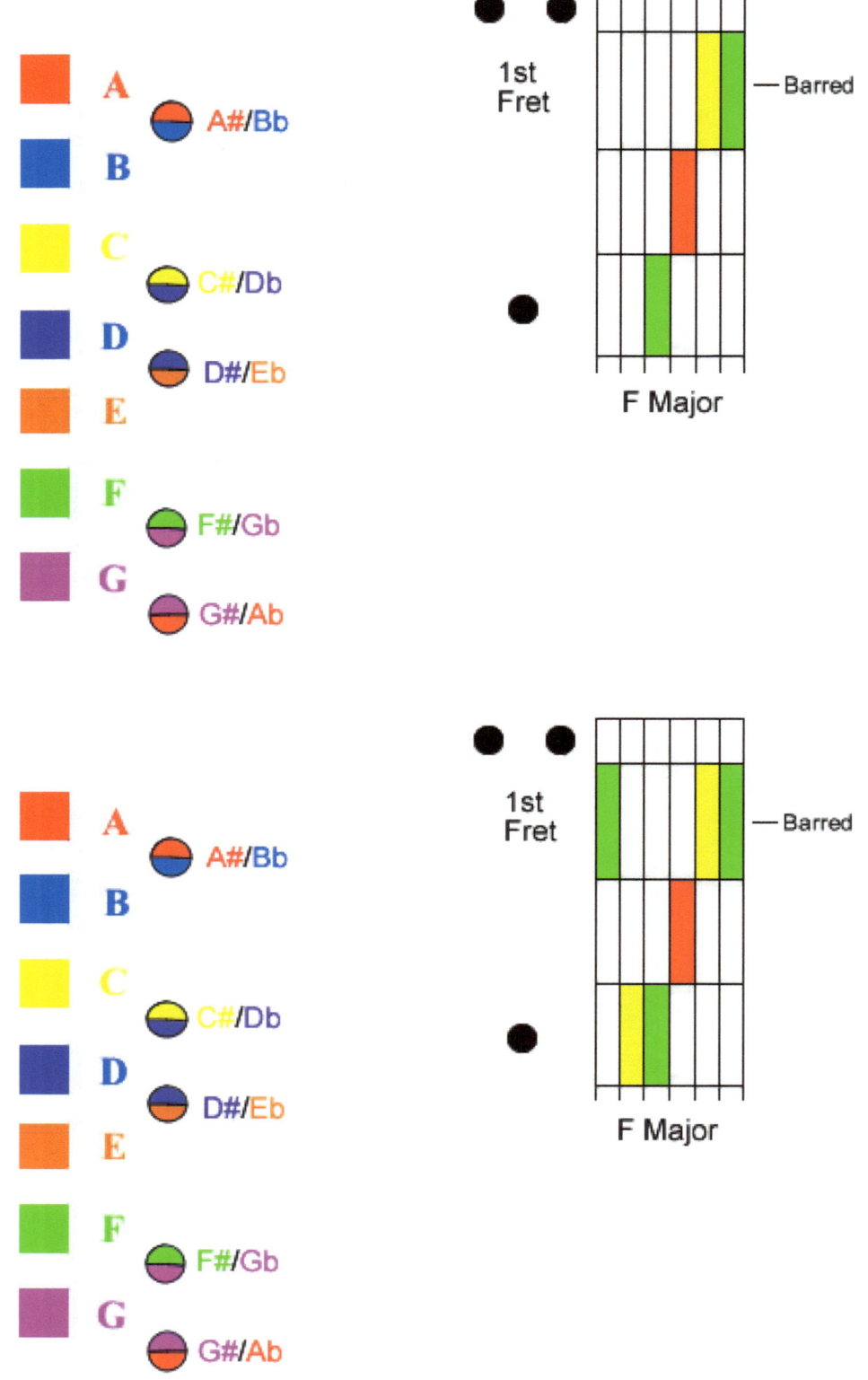

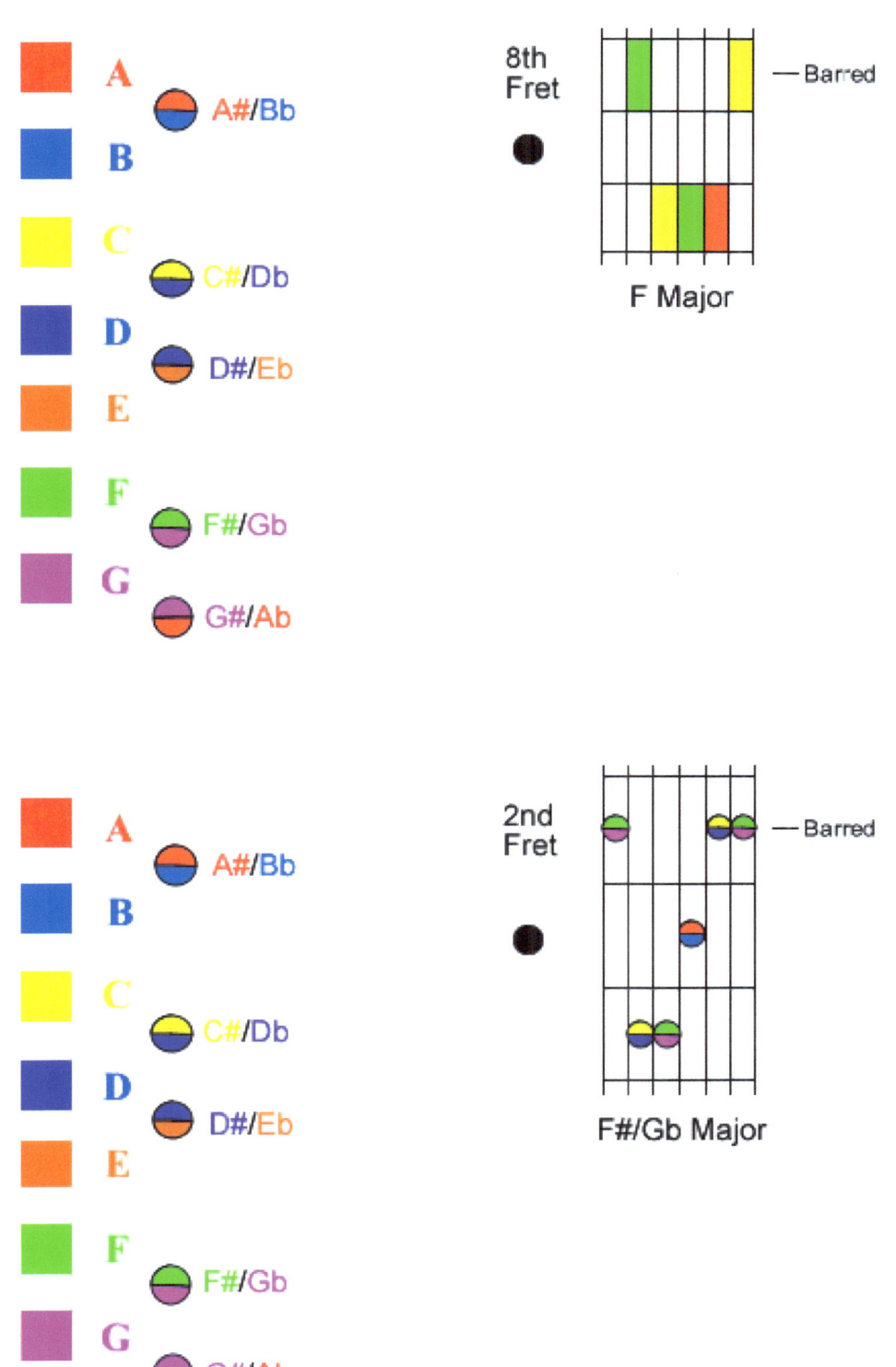

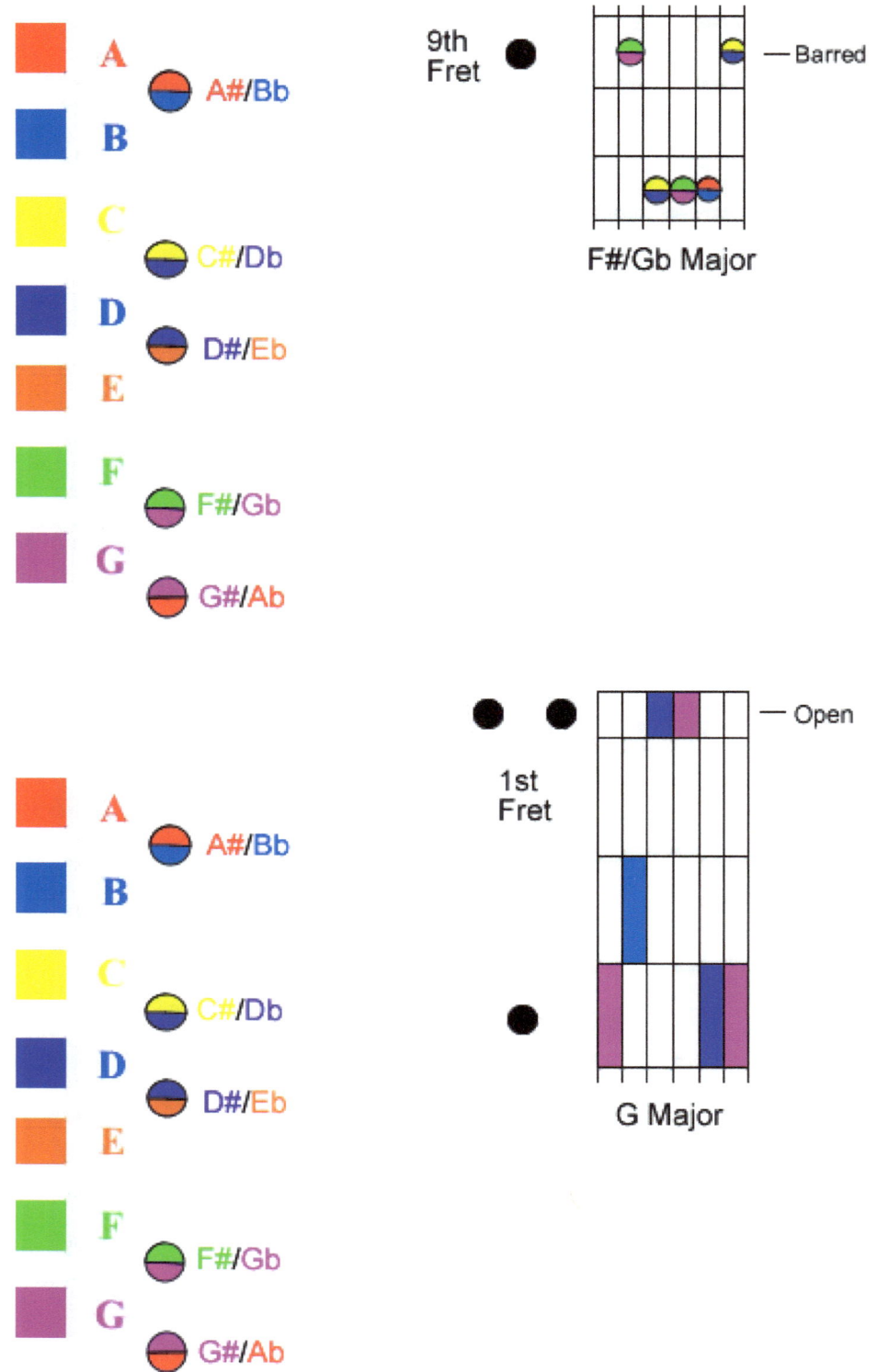

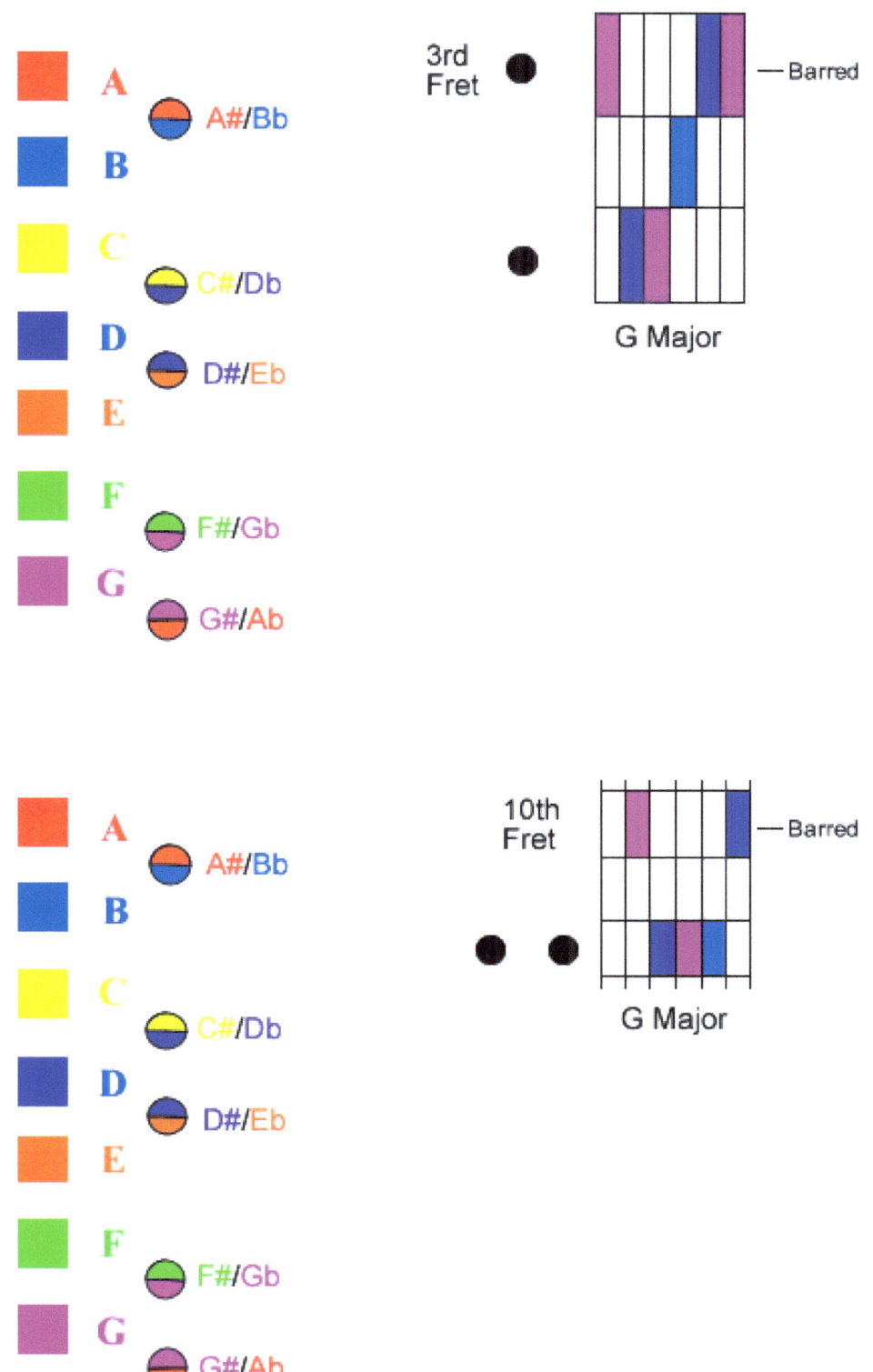

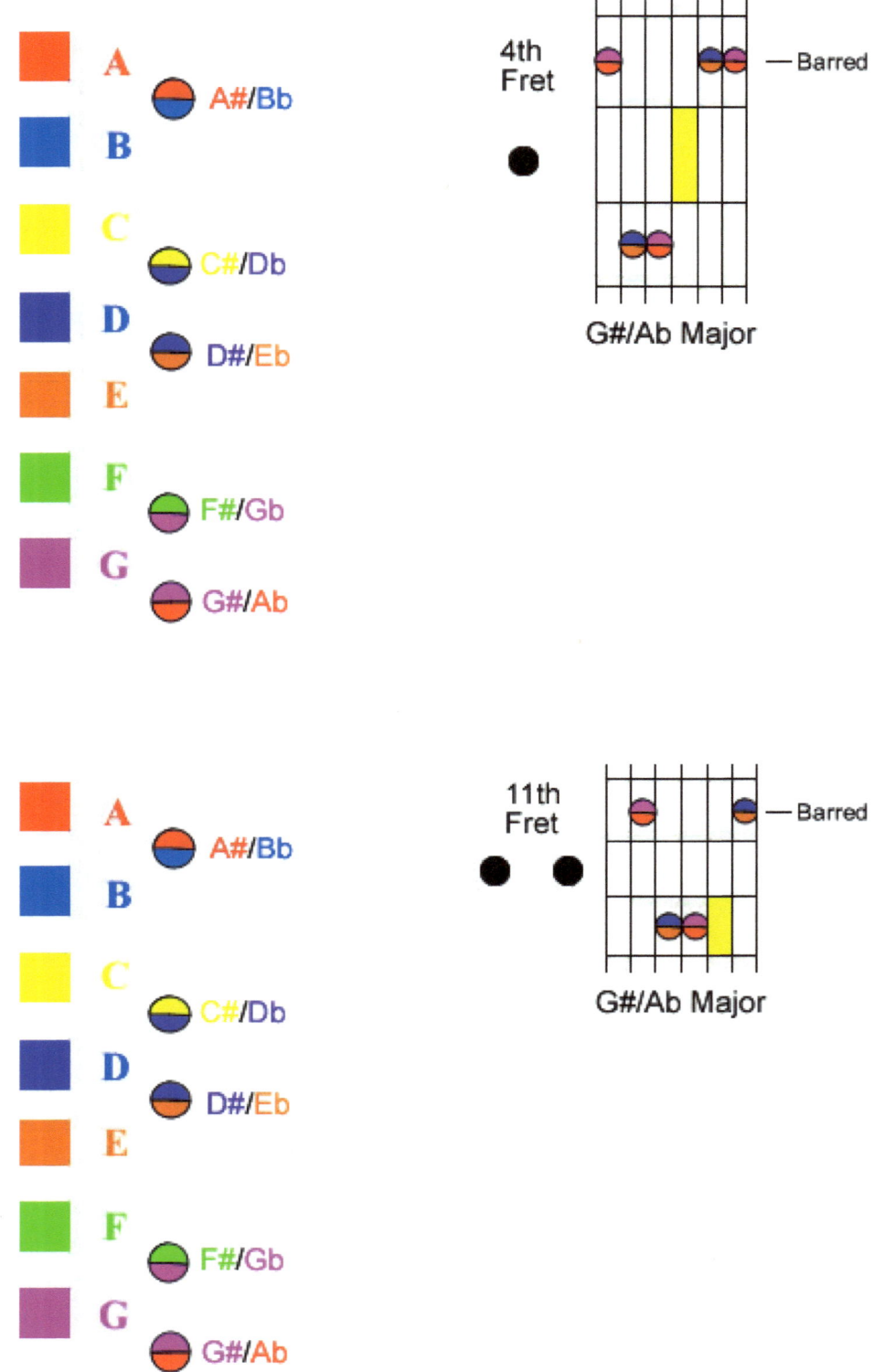

-Minor Chords-

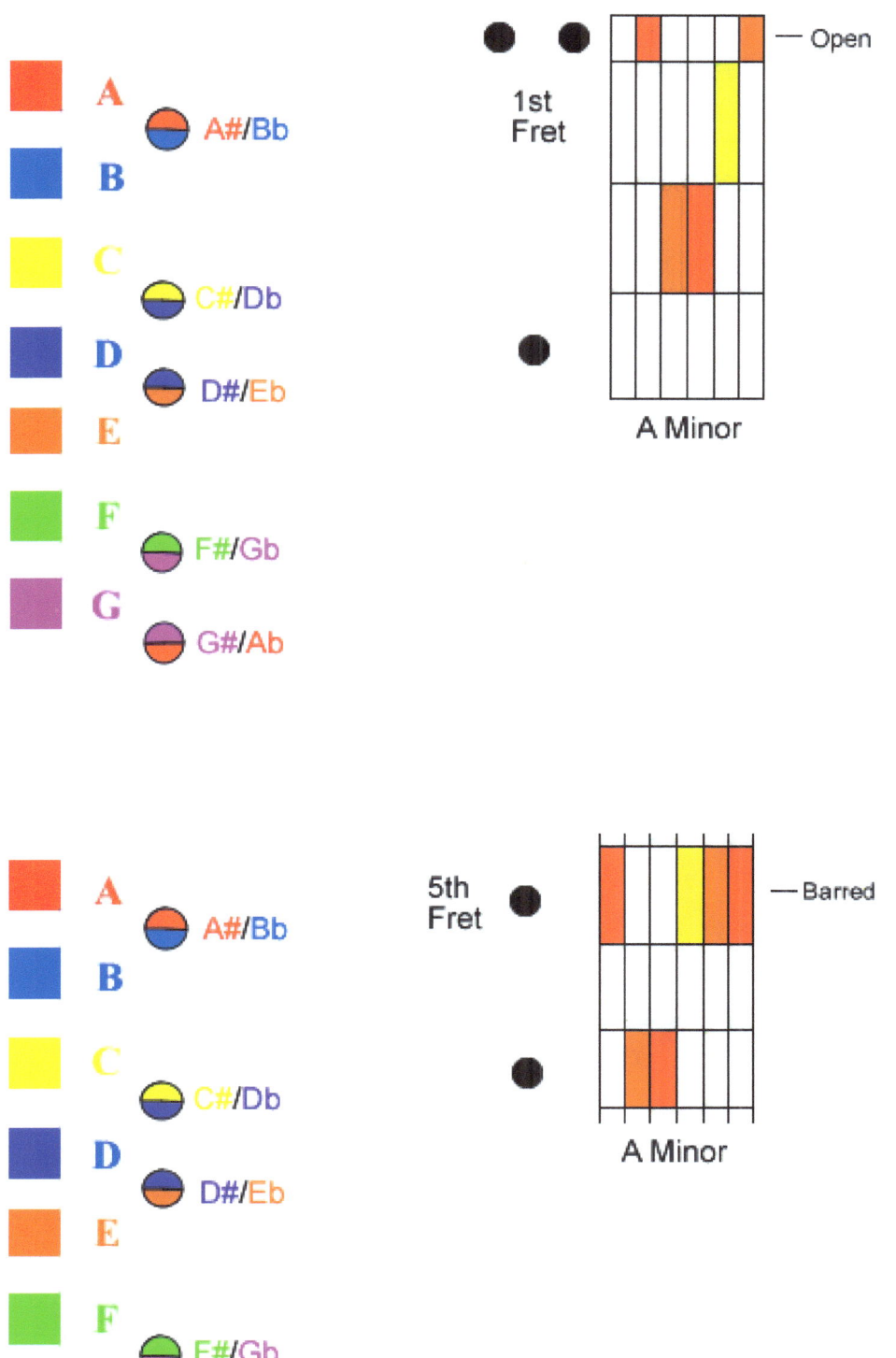

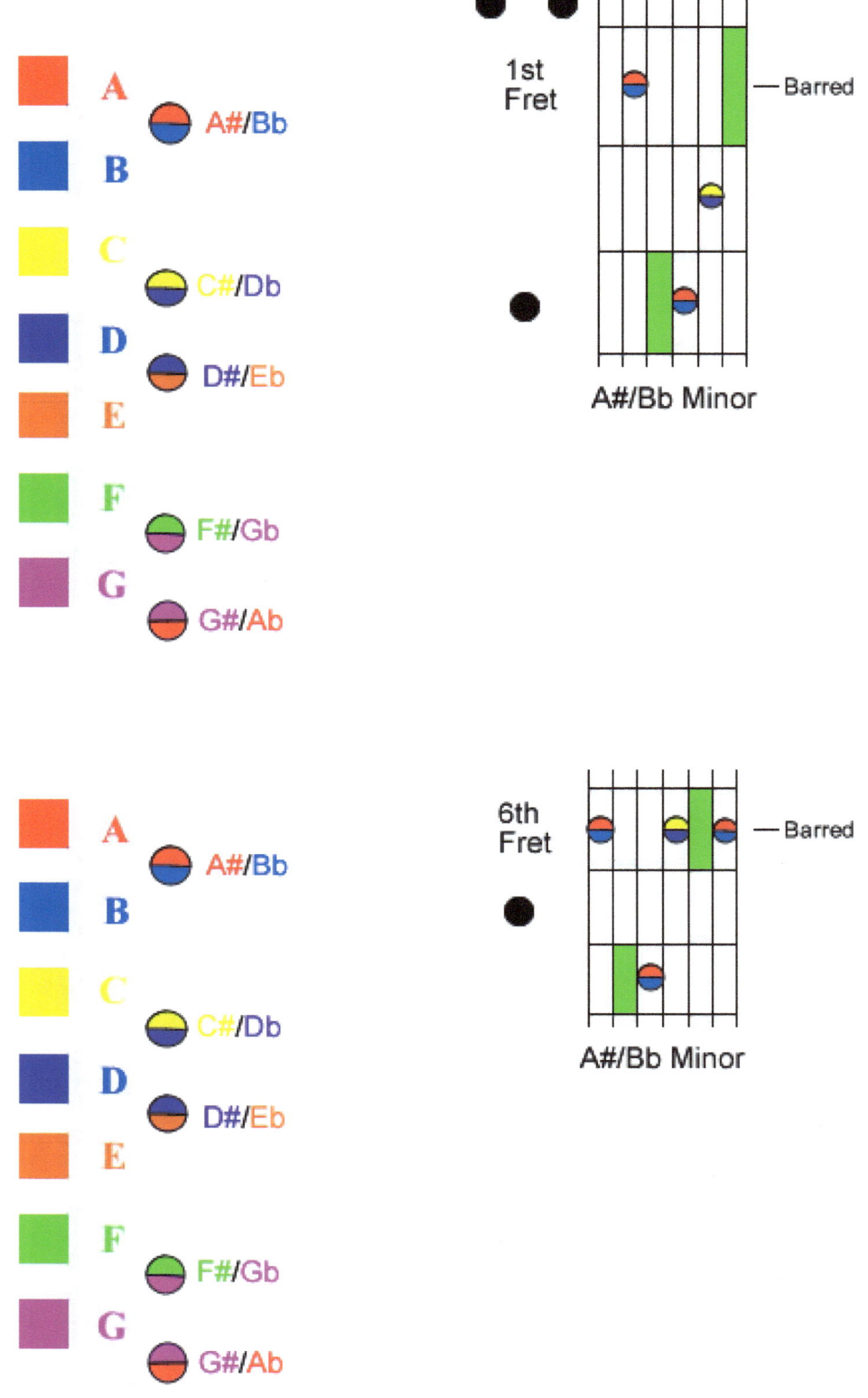

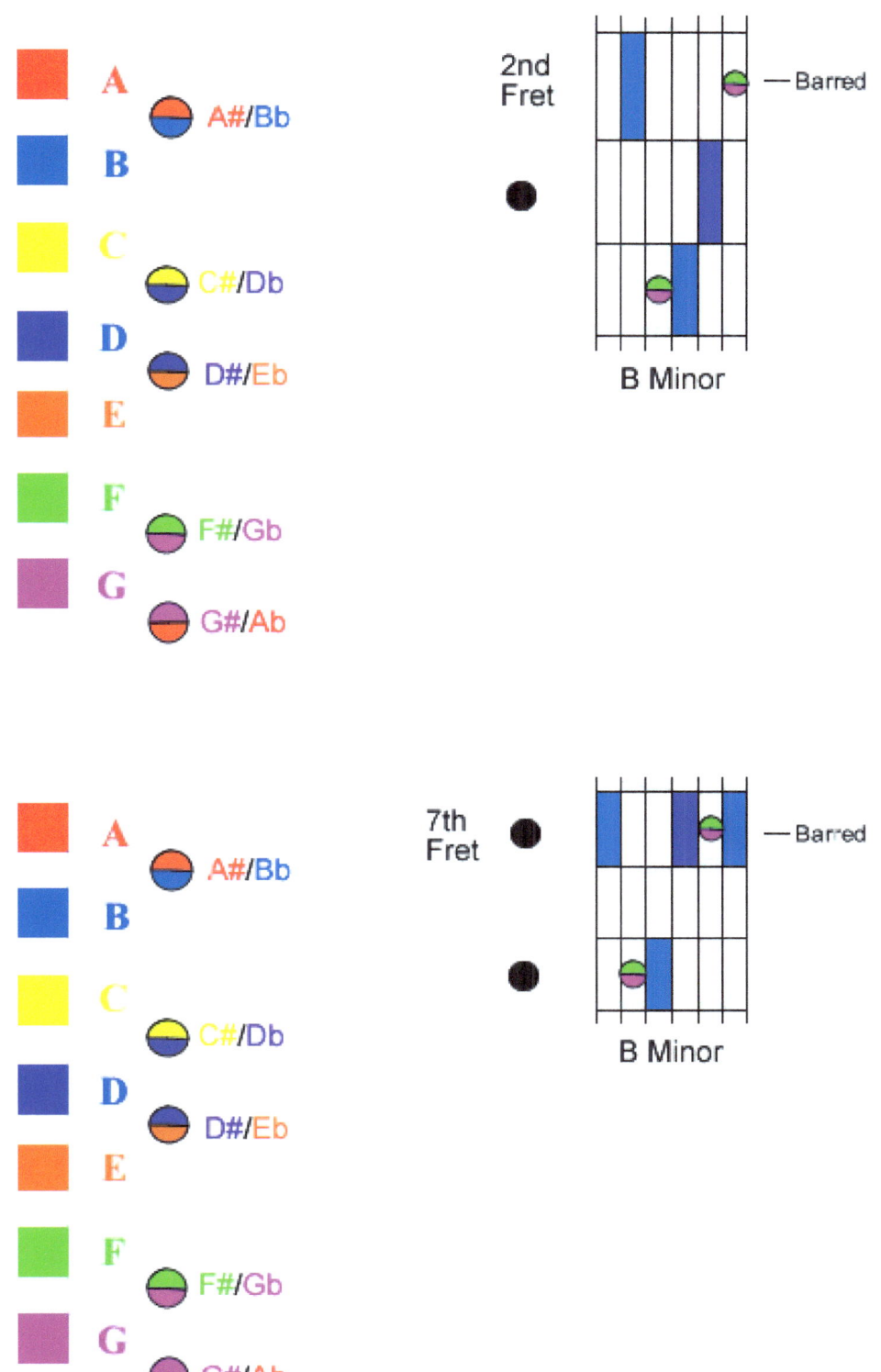

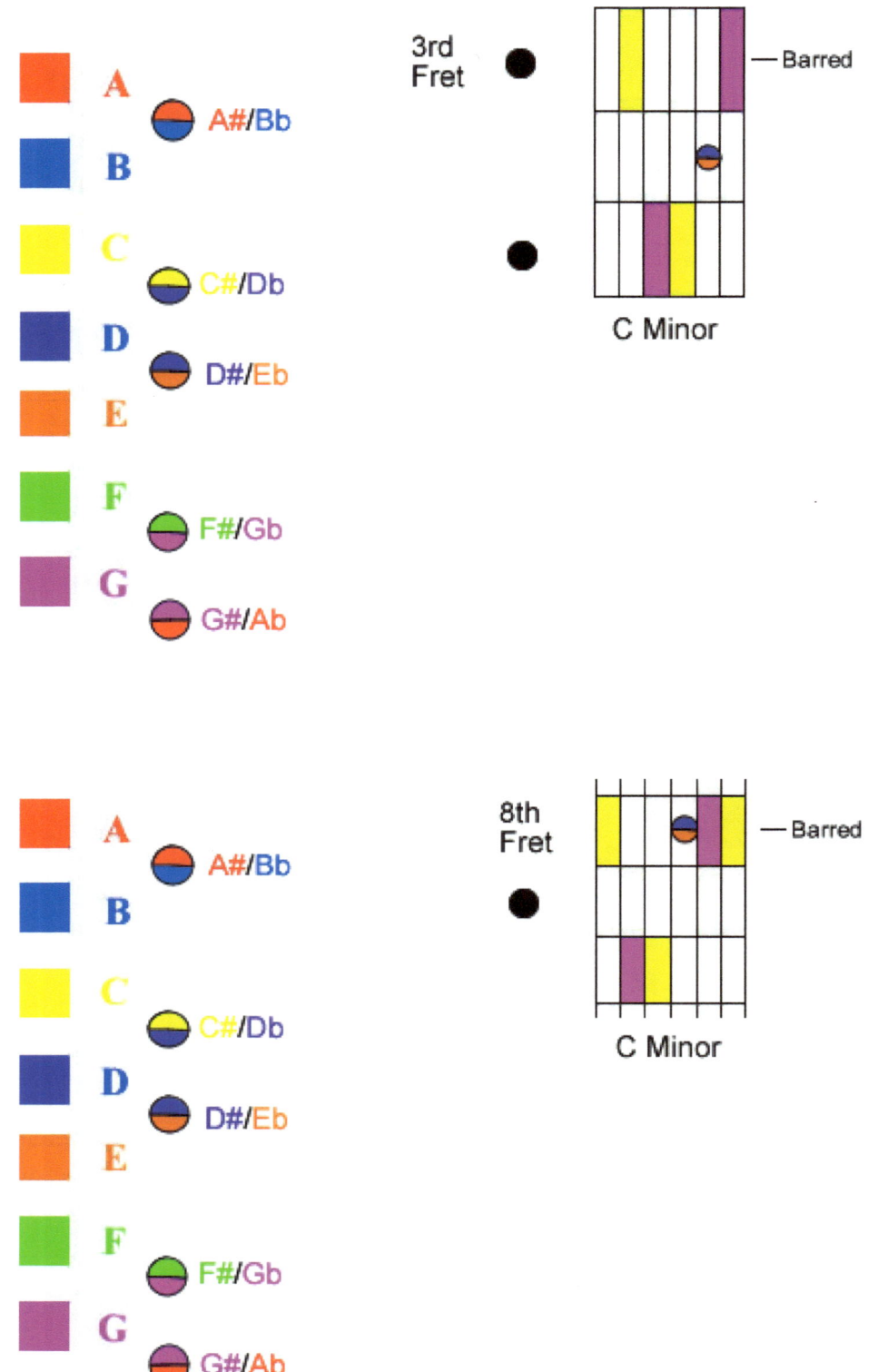

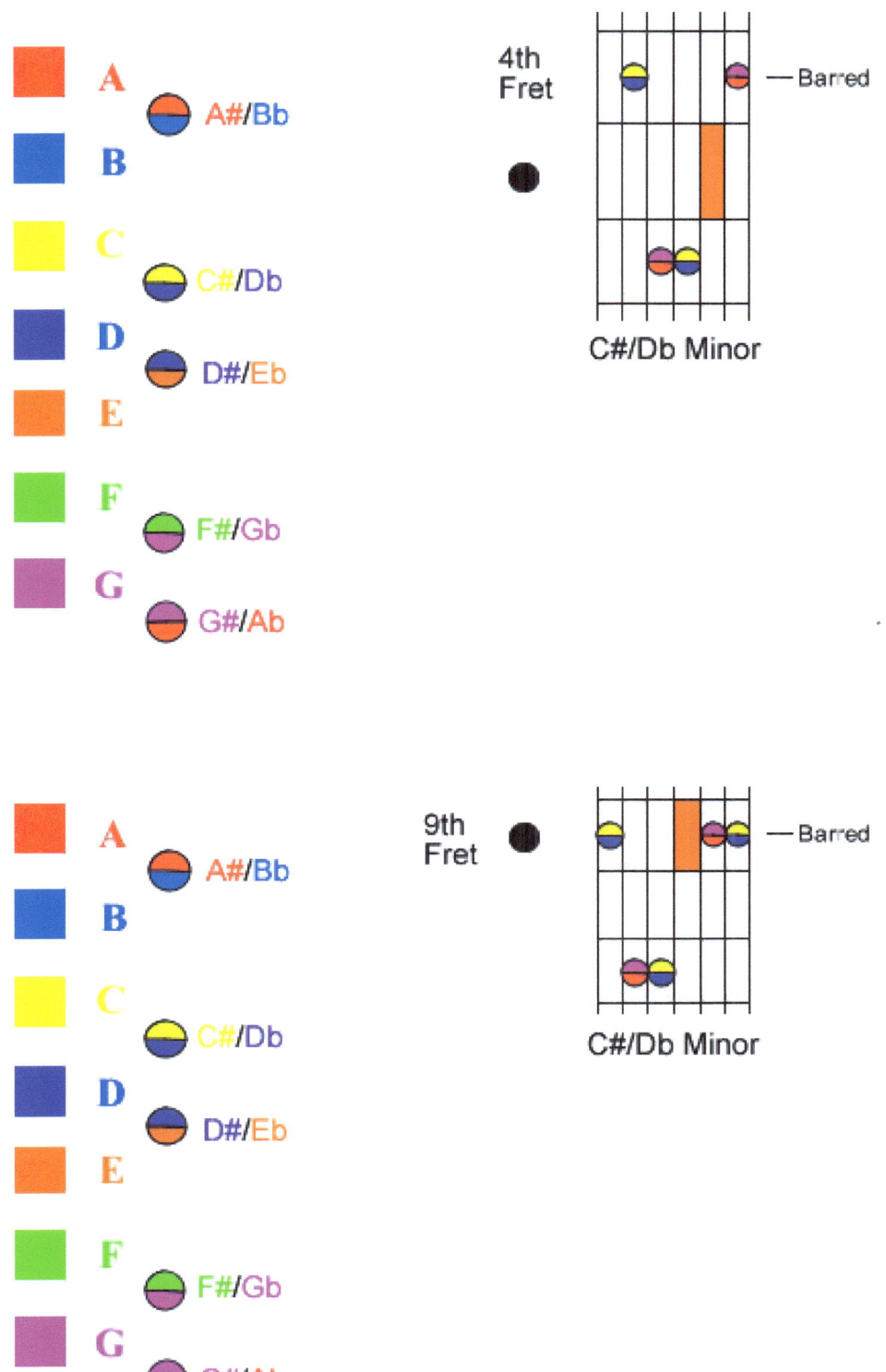

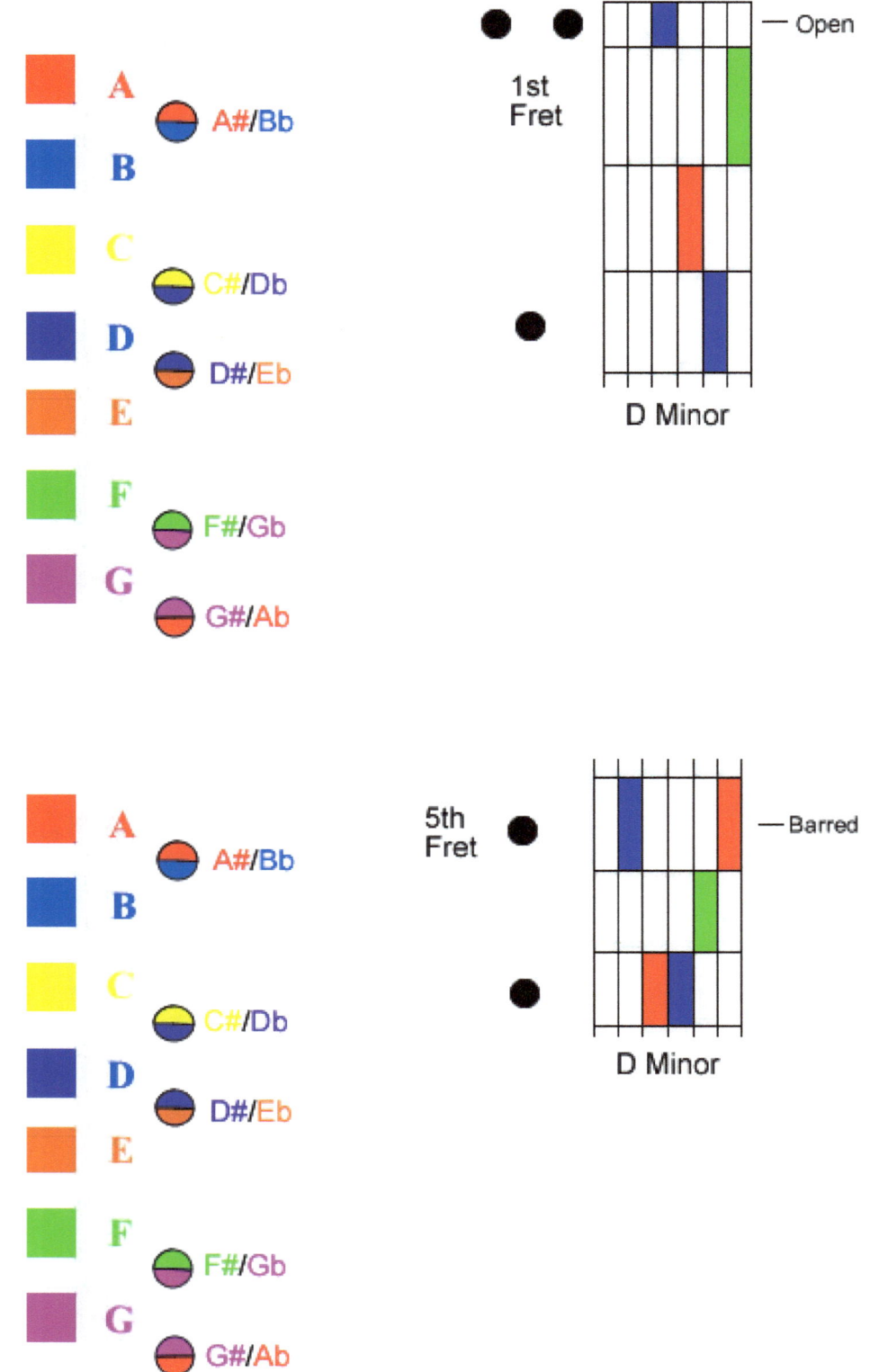

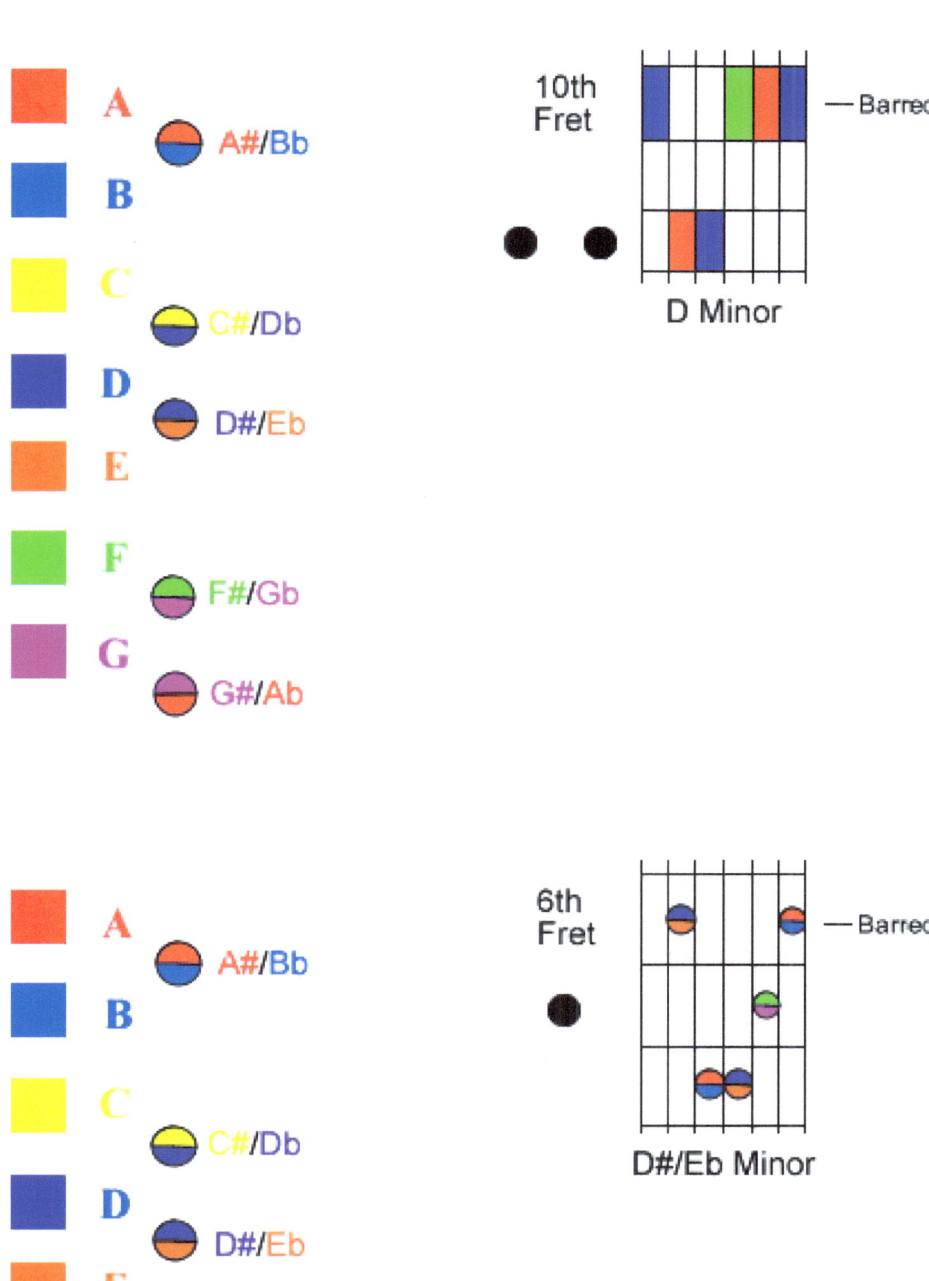

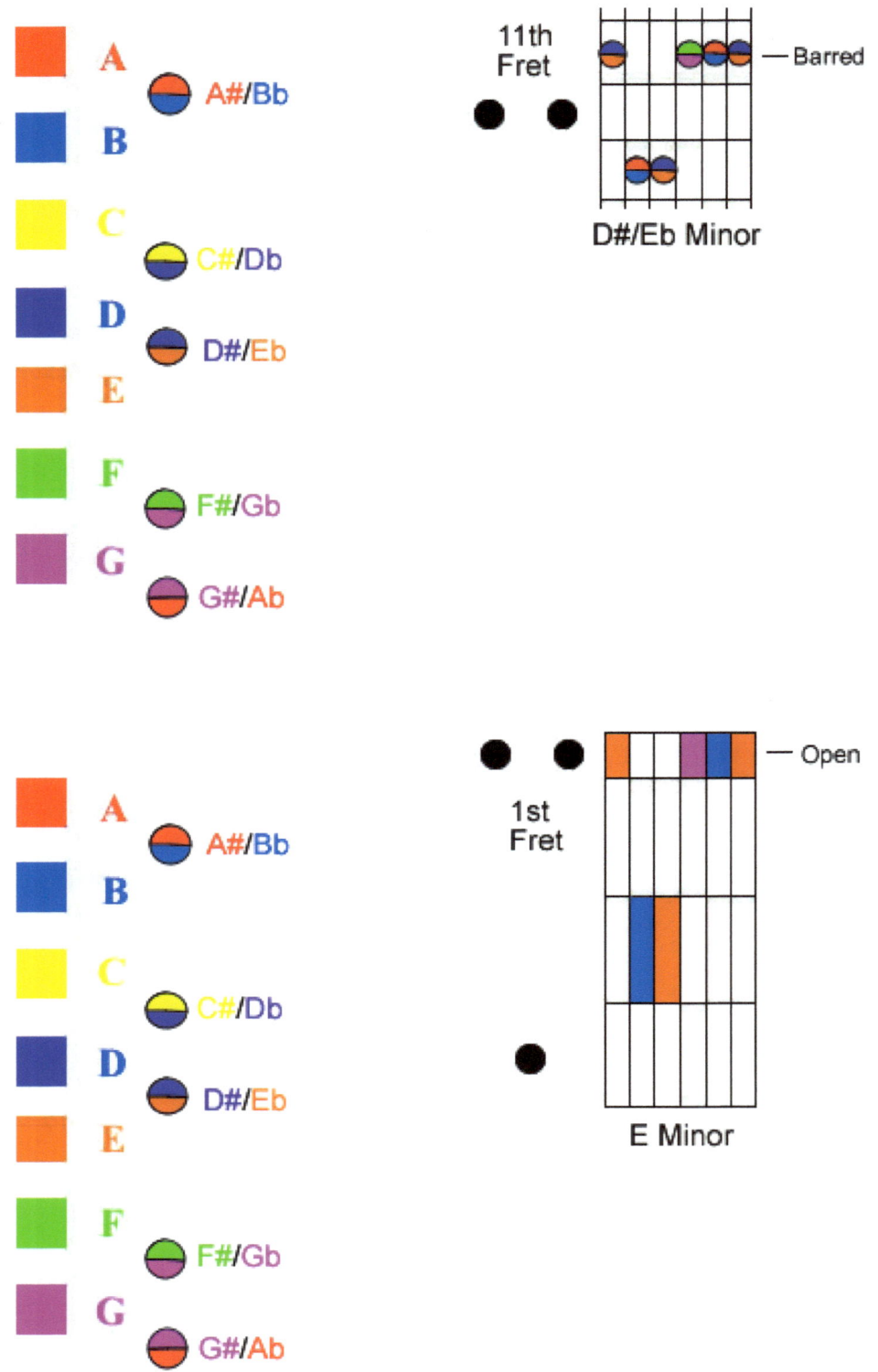

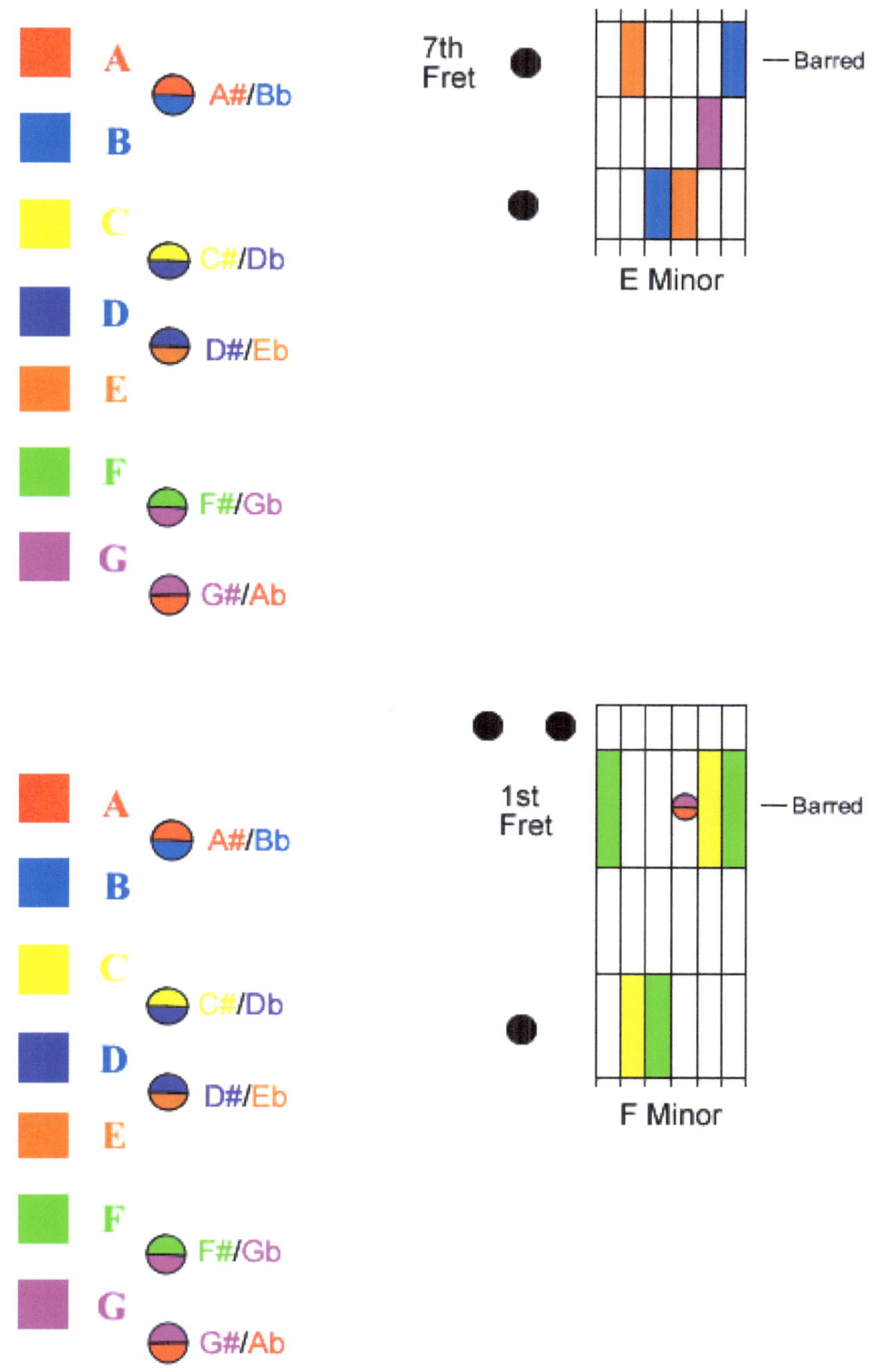

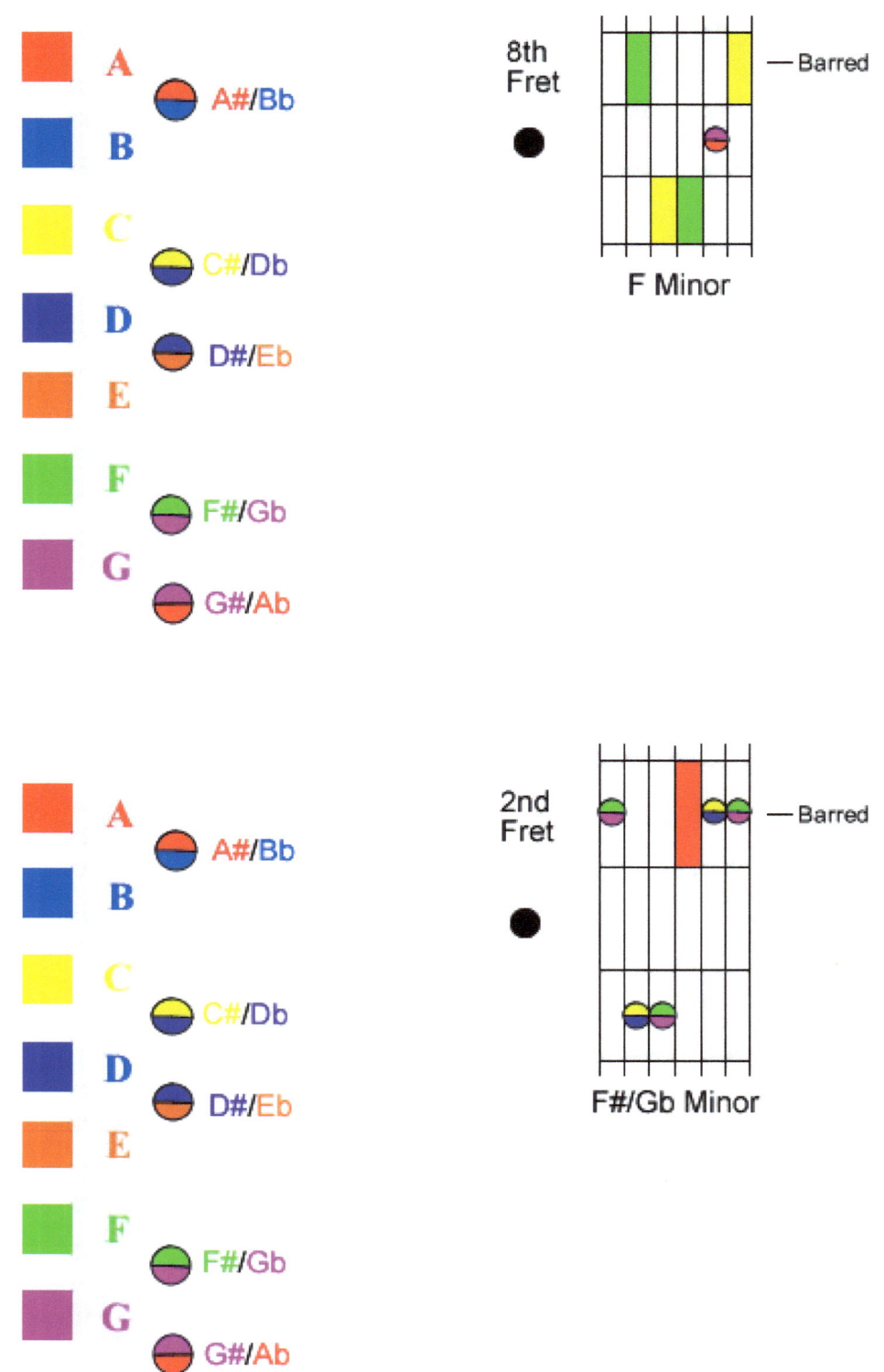

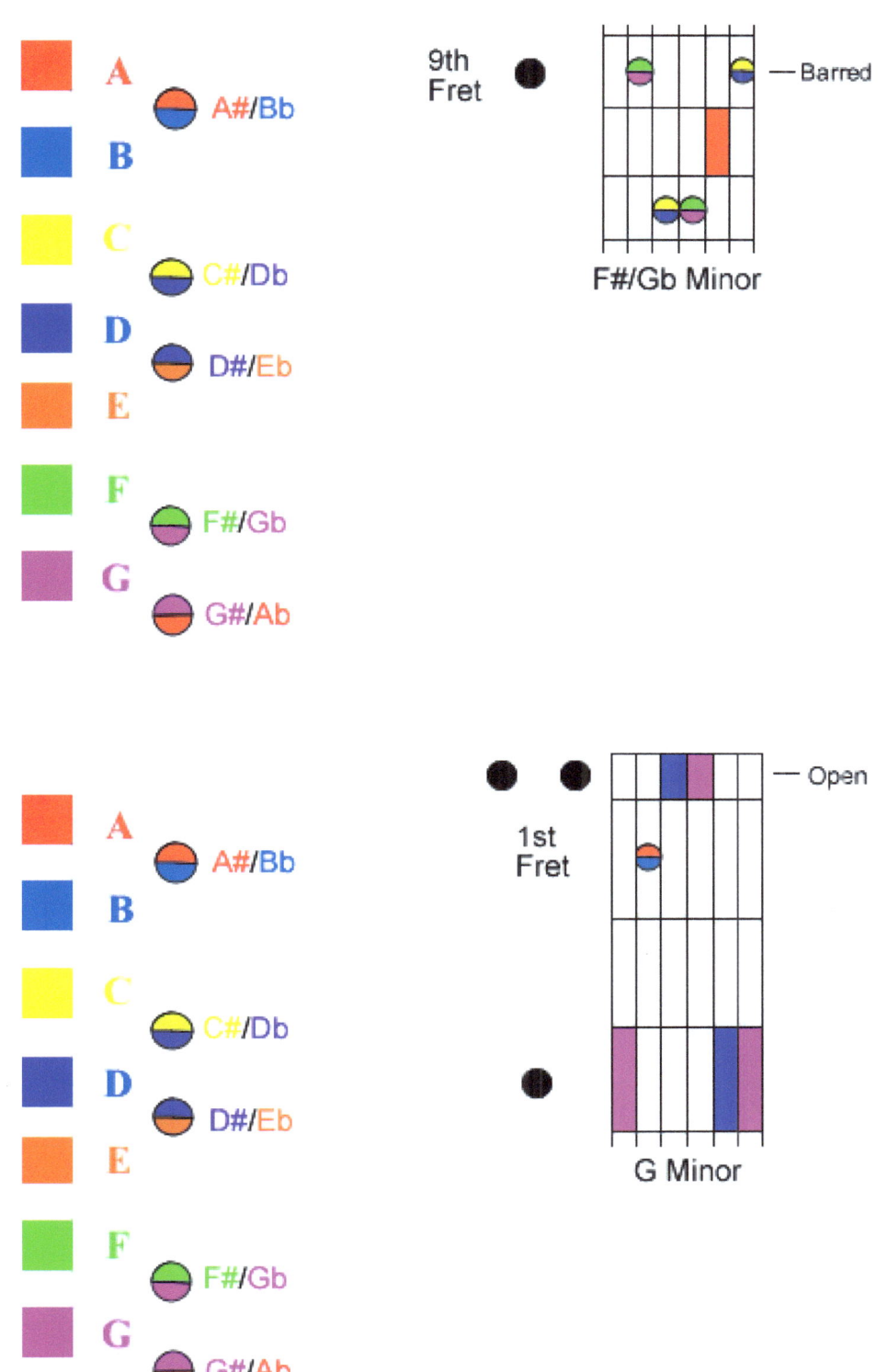

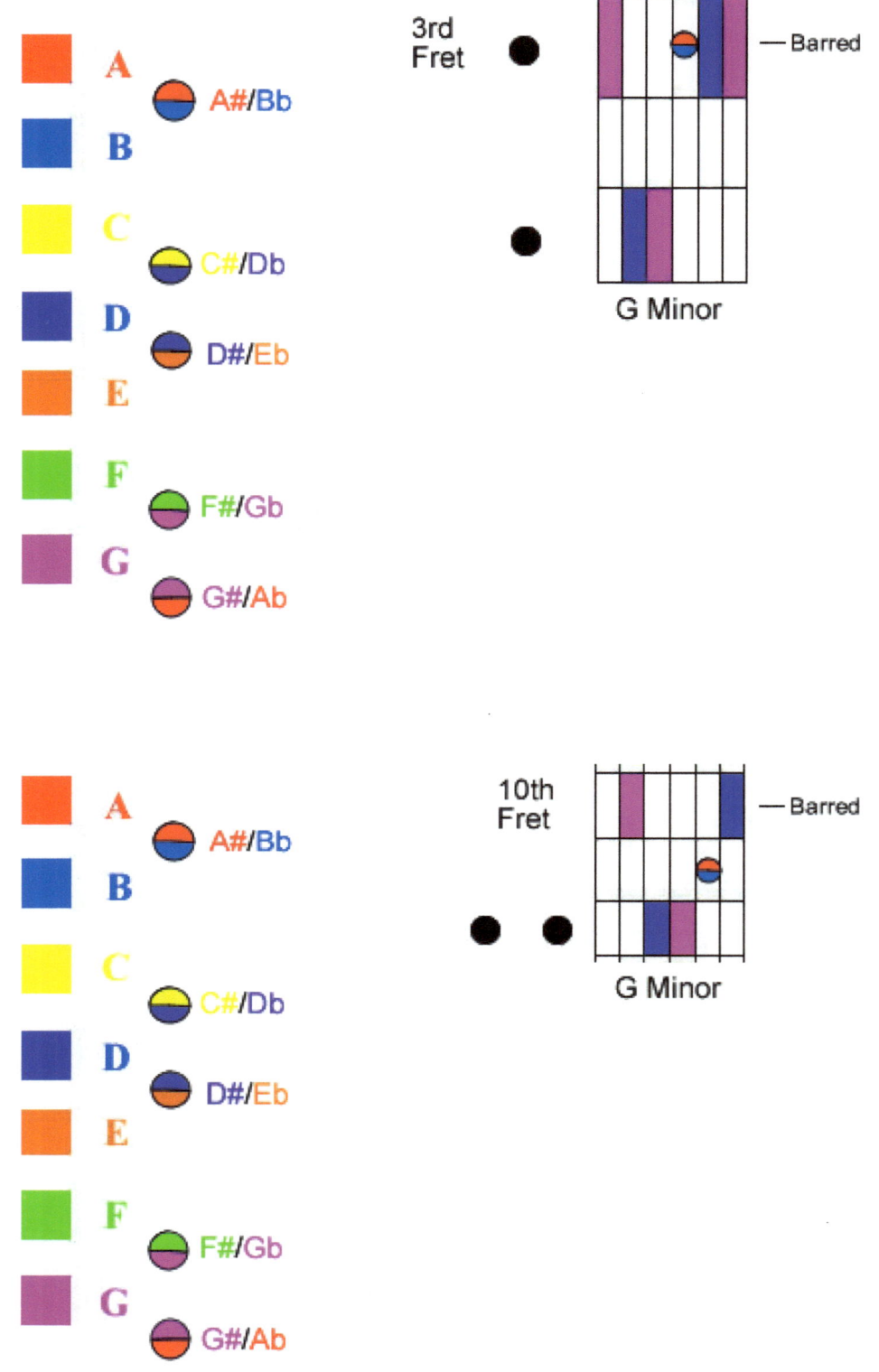

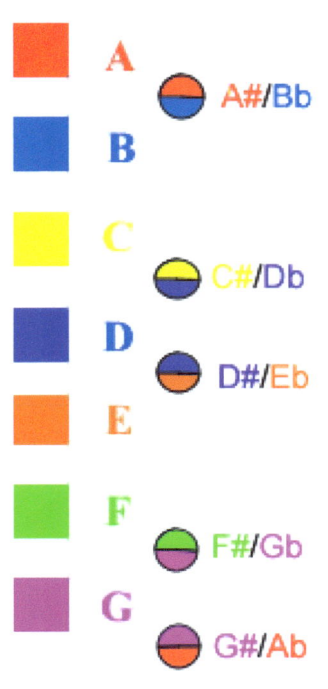
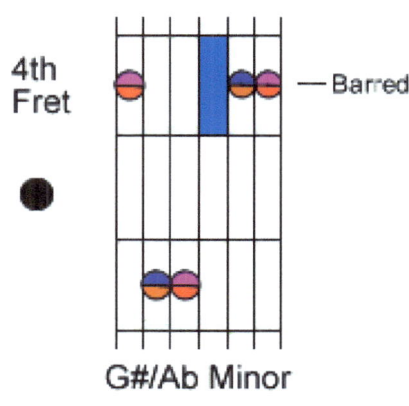

G#/Ab Minor

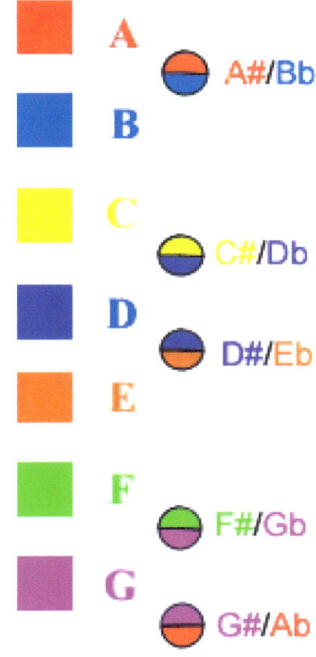
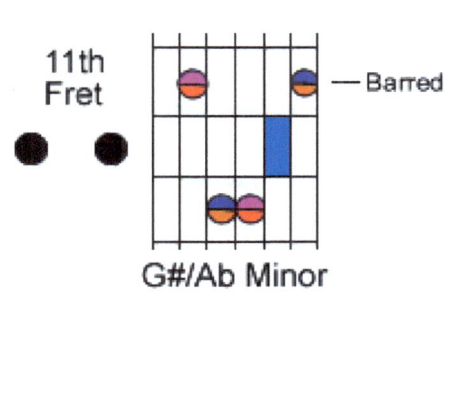

G#/Ab Minor

70

-Dominant 7th Chords-

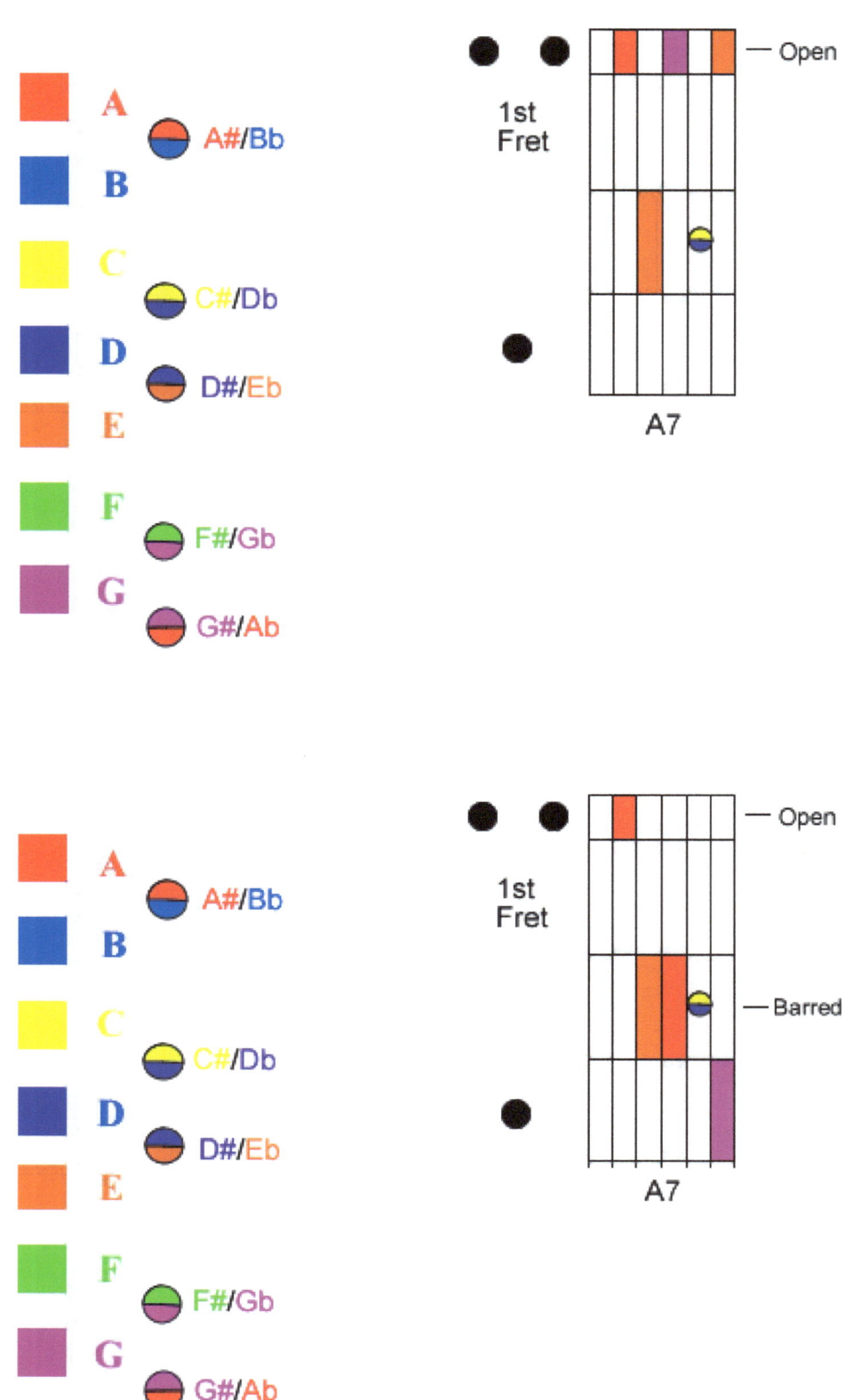

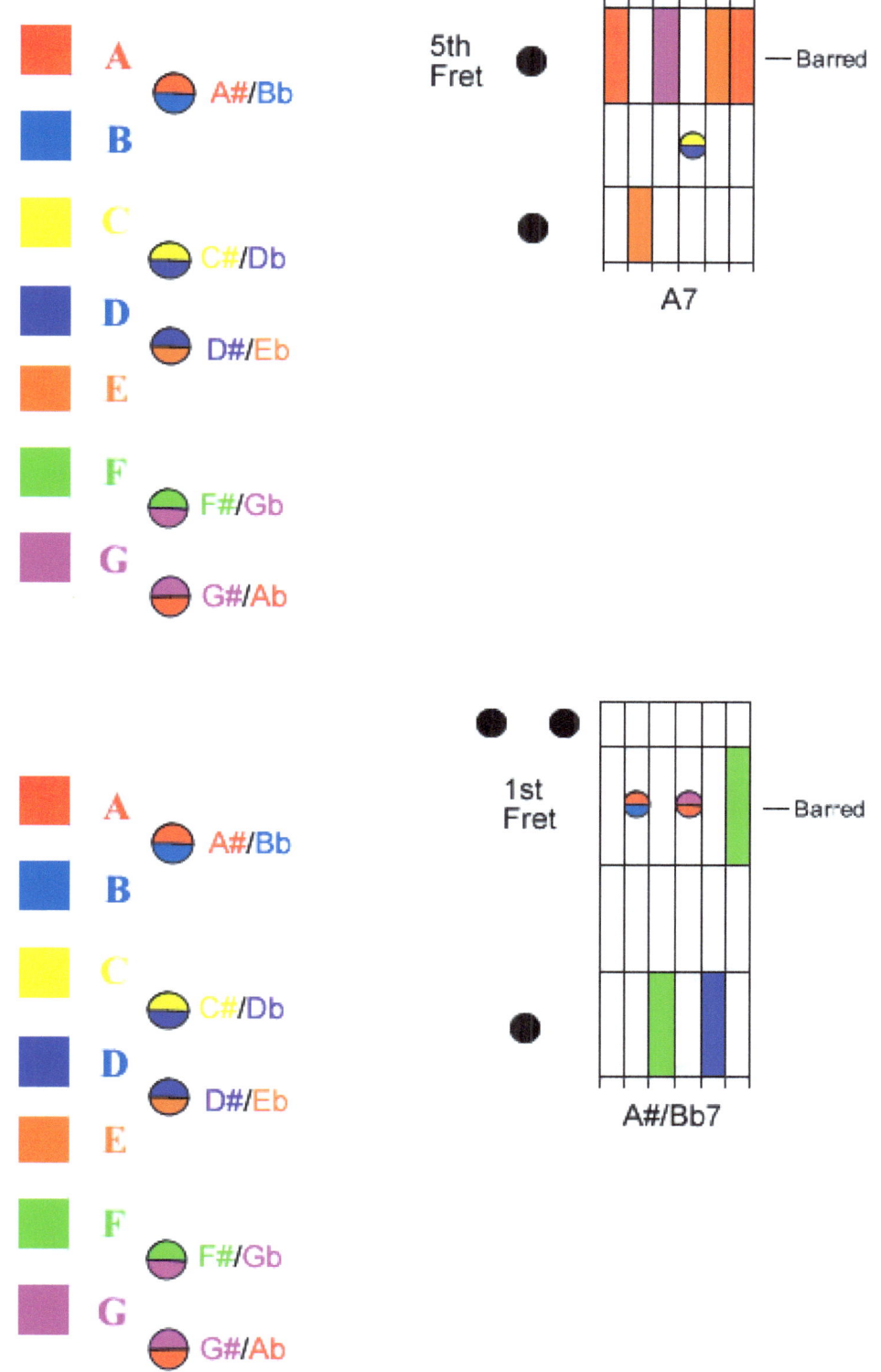

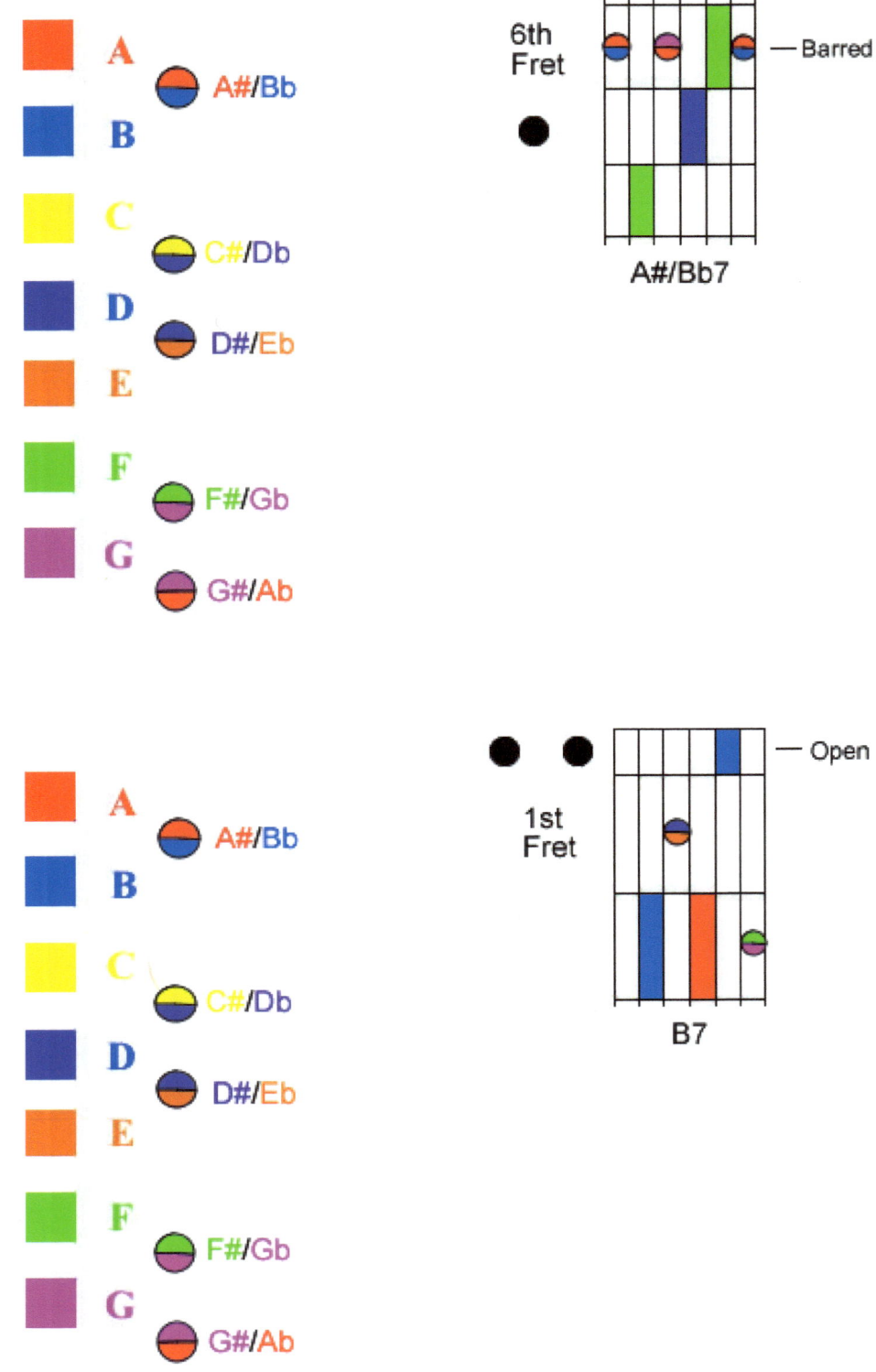

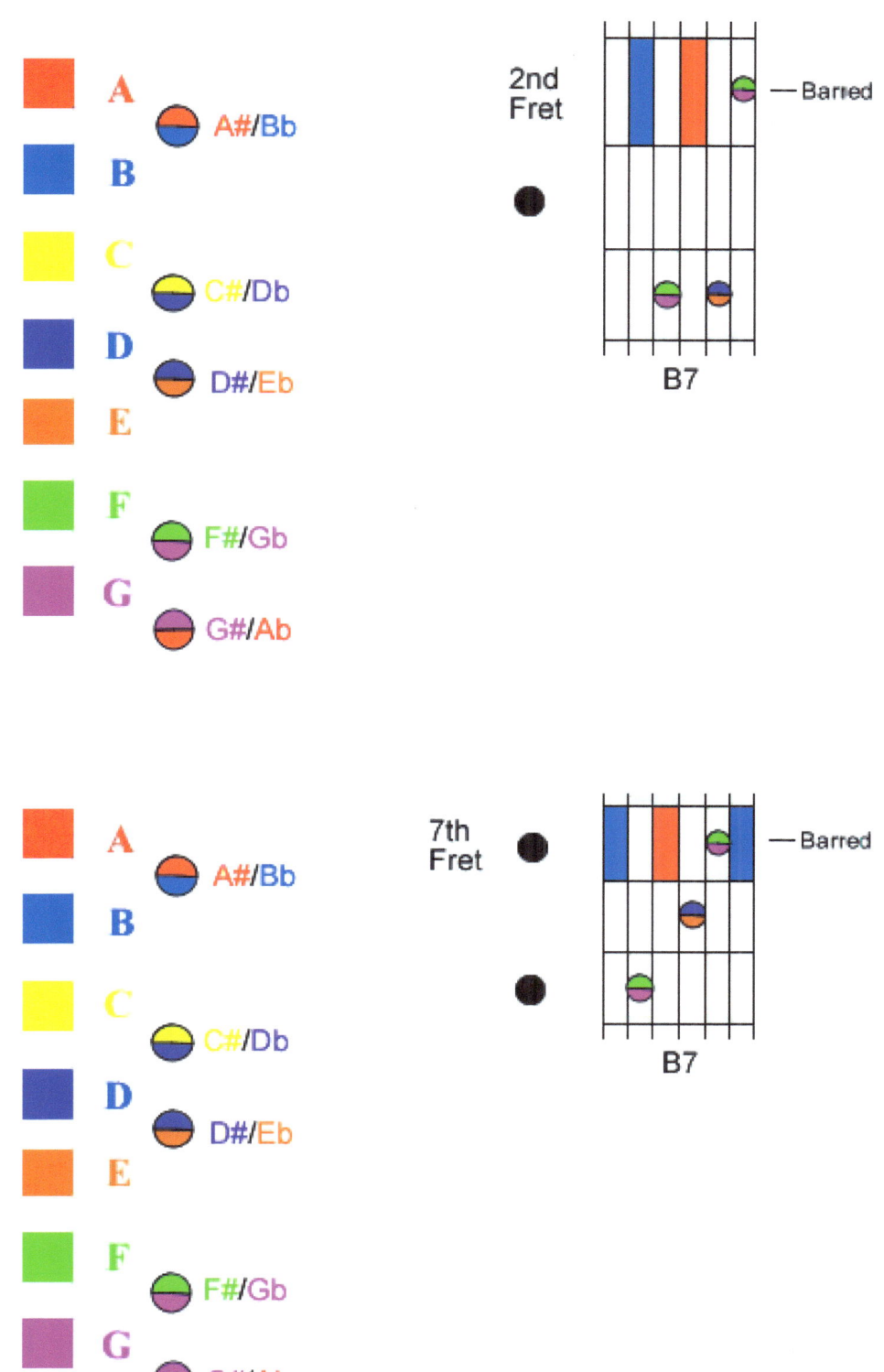

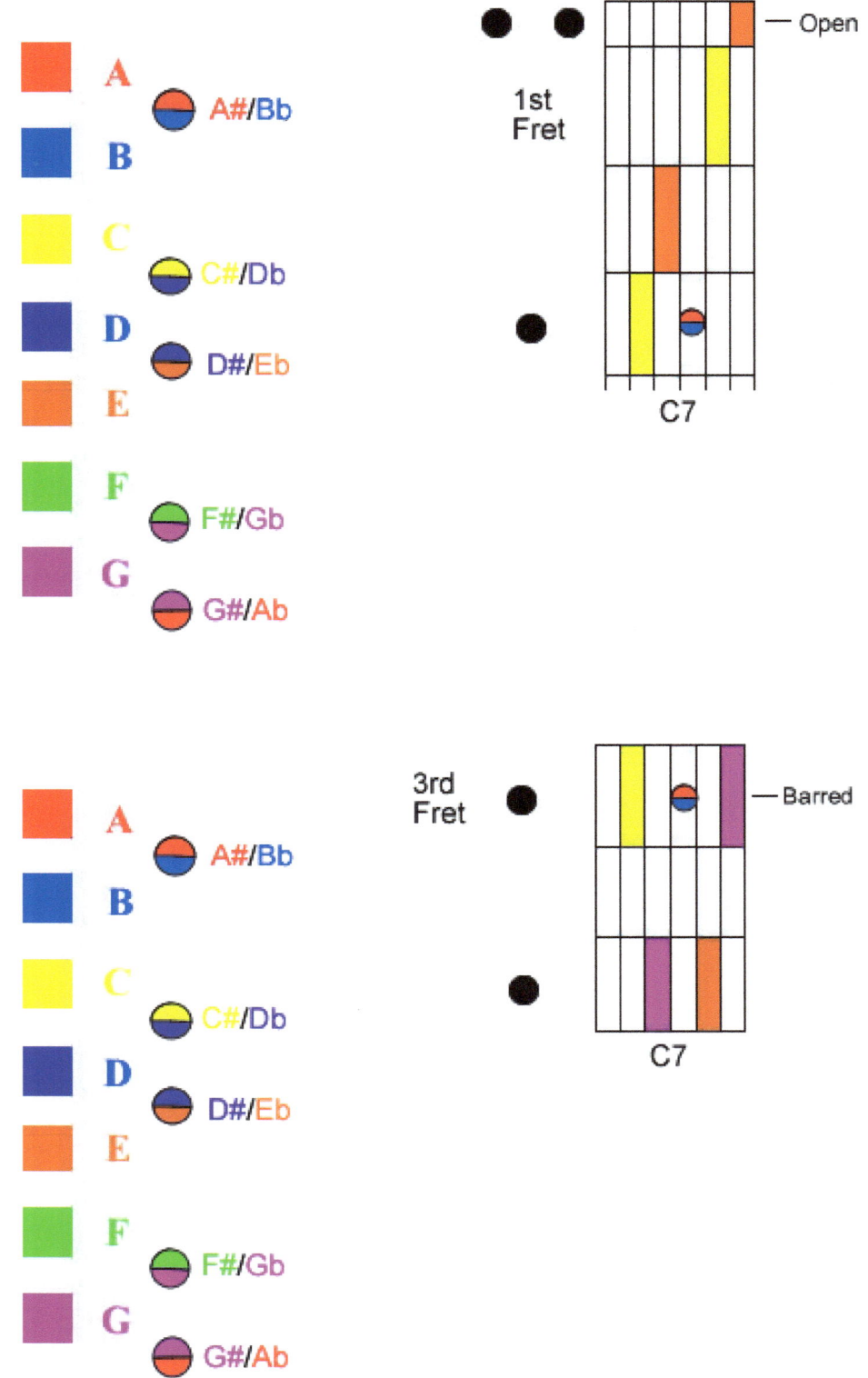

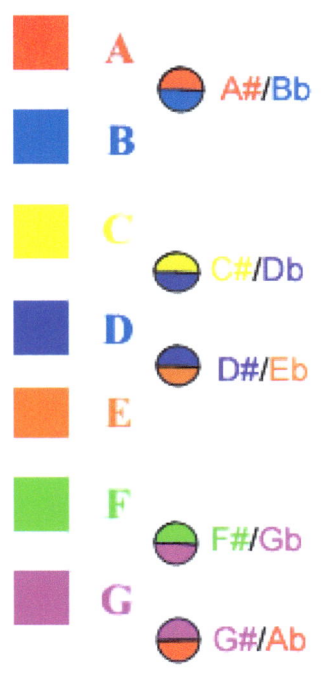
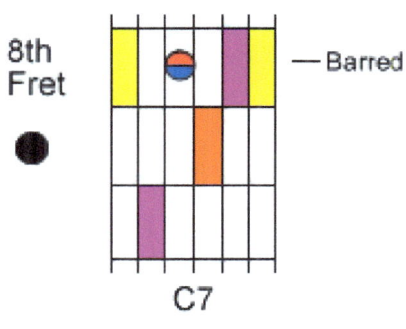

C7

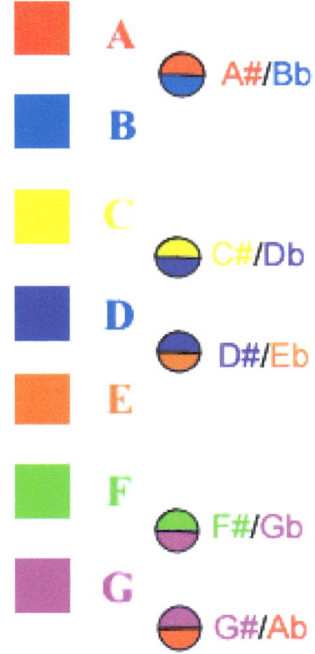
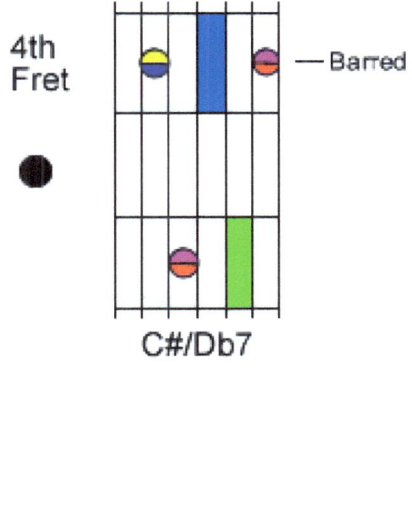

C#/Db7

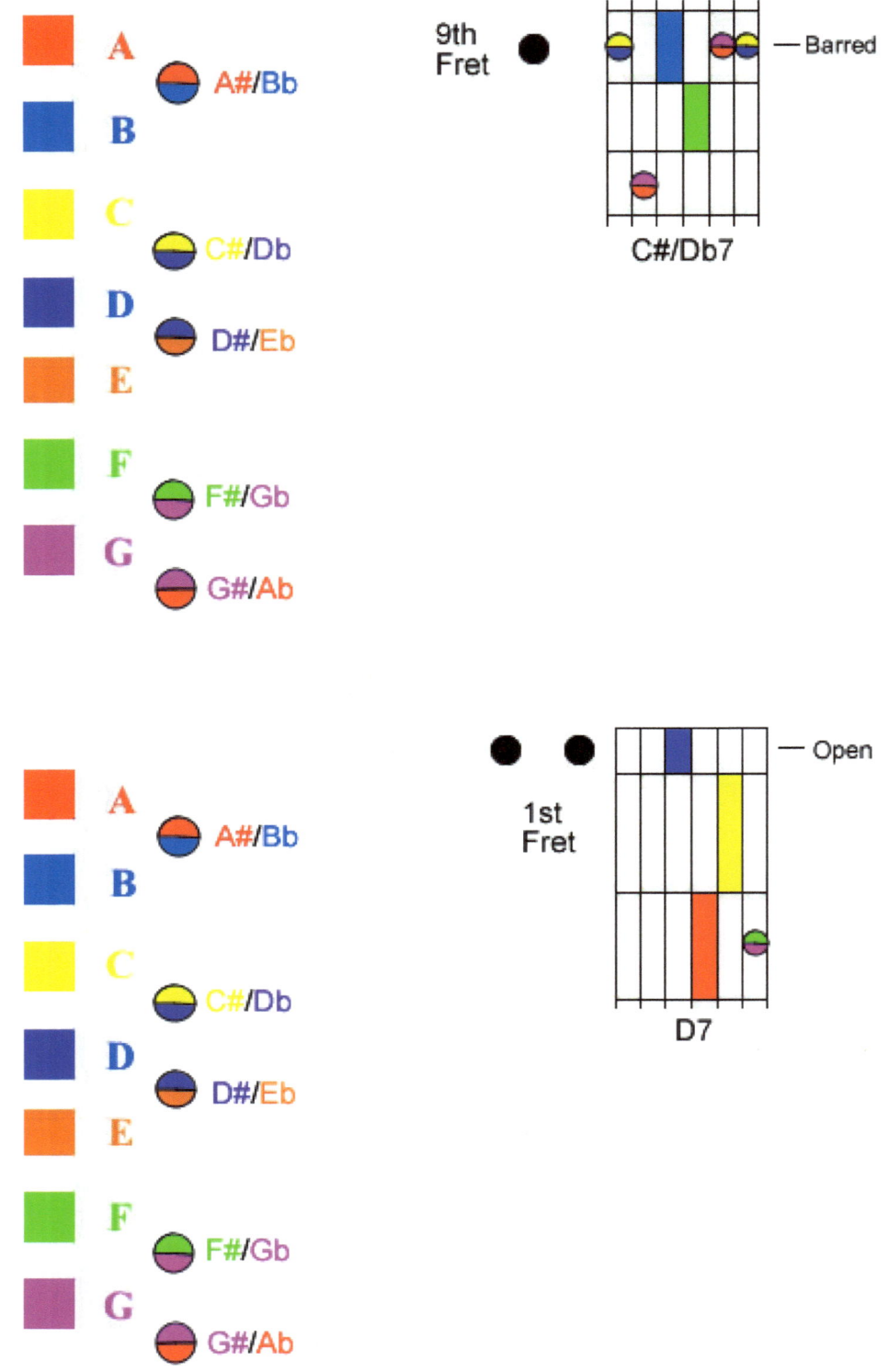

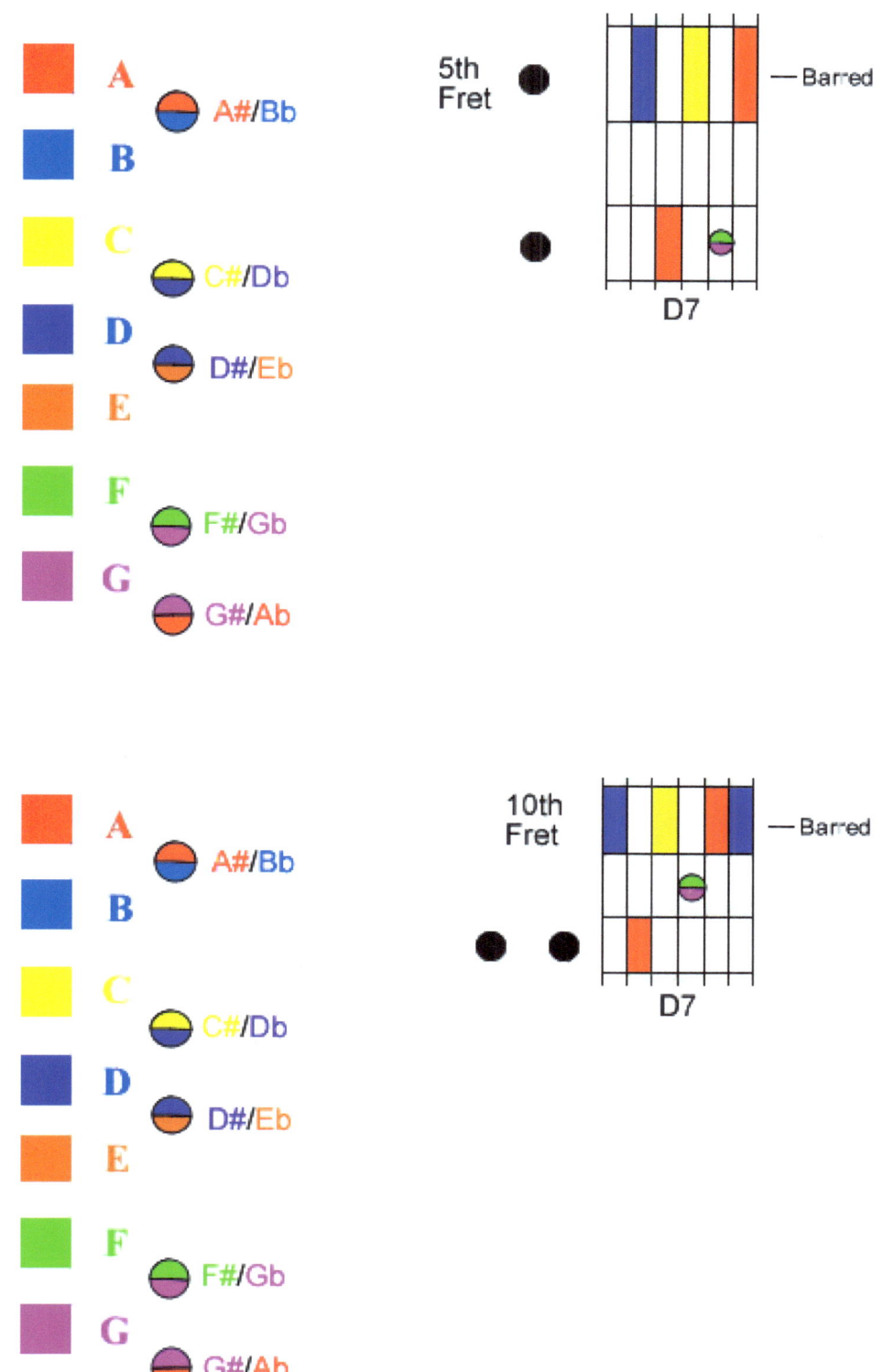

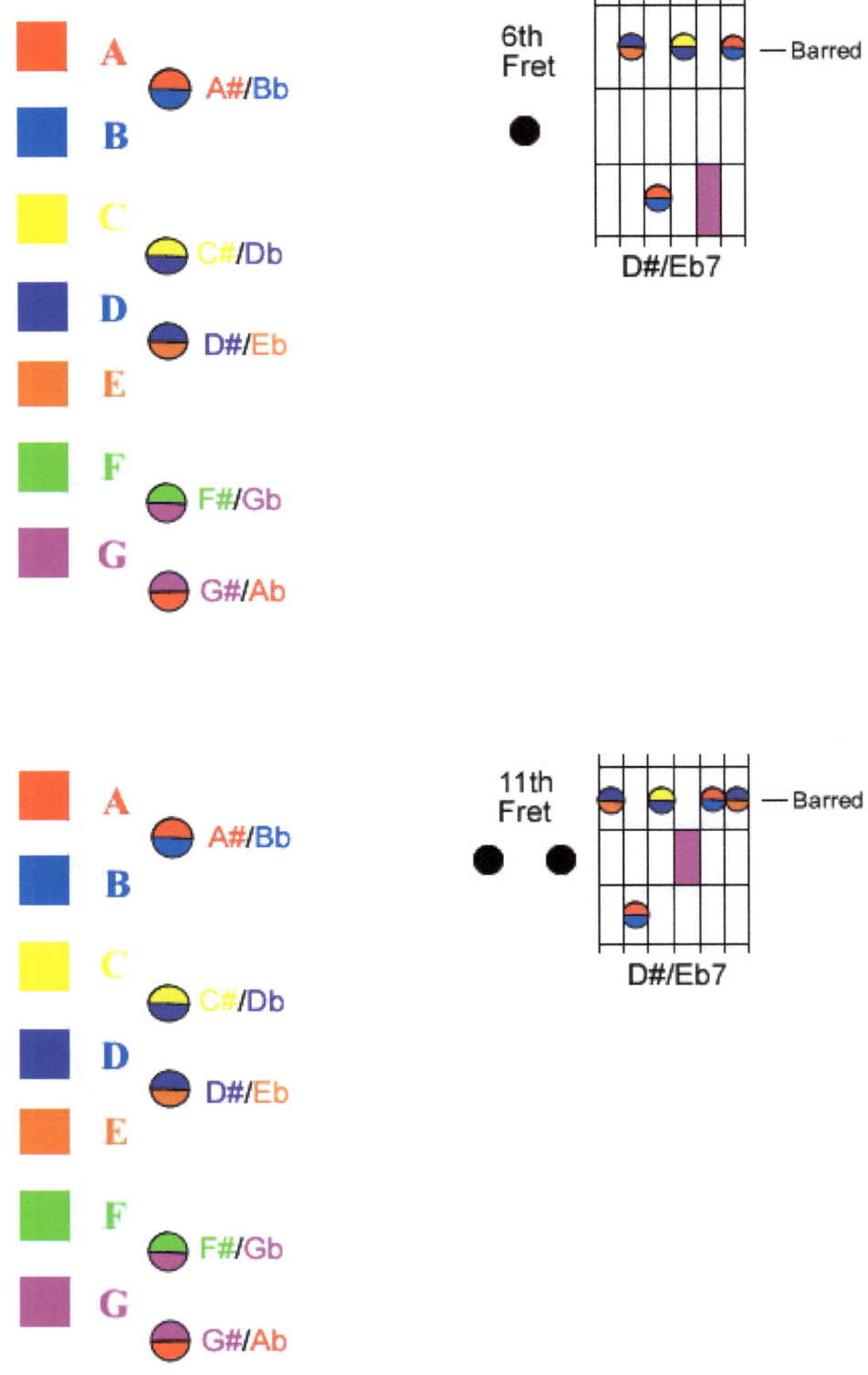

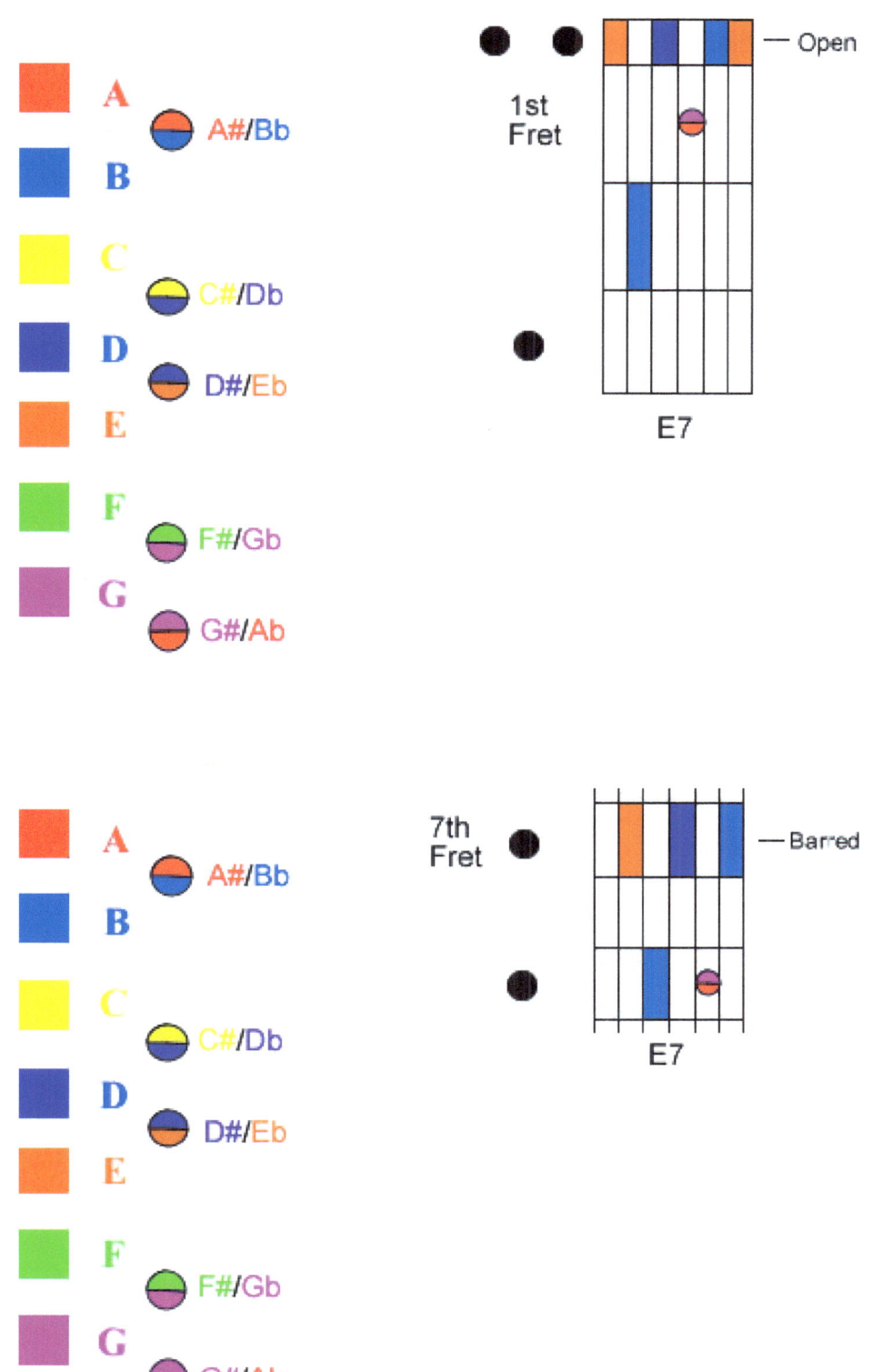

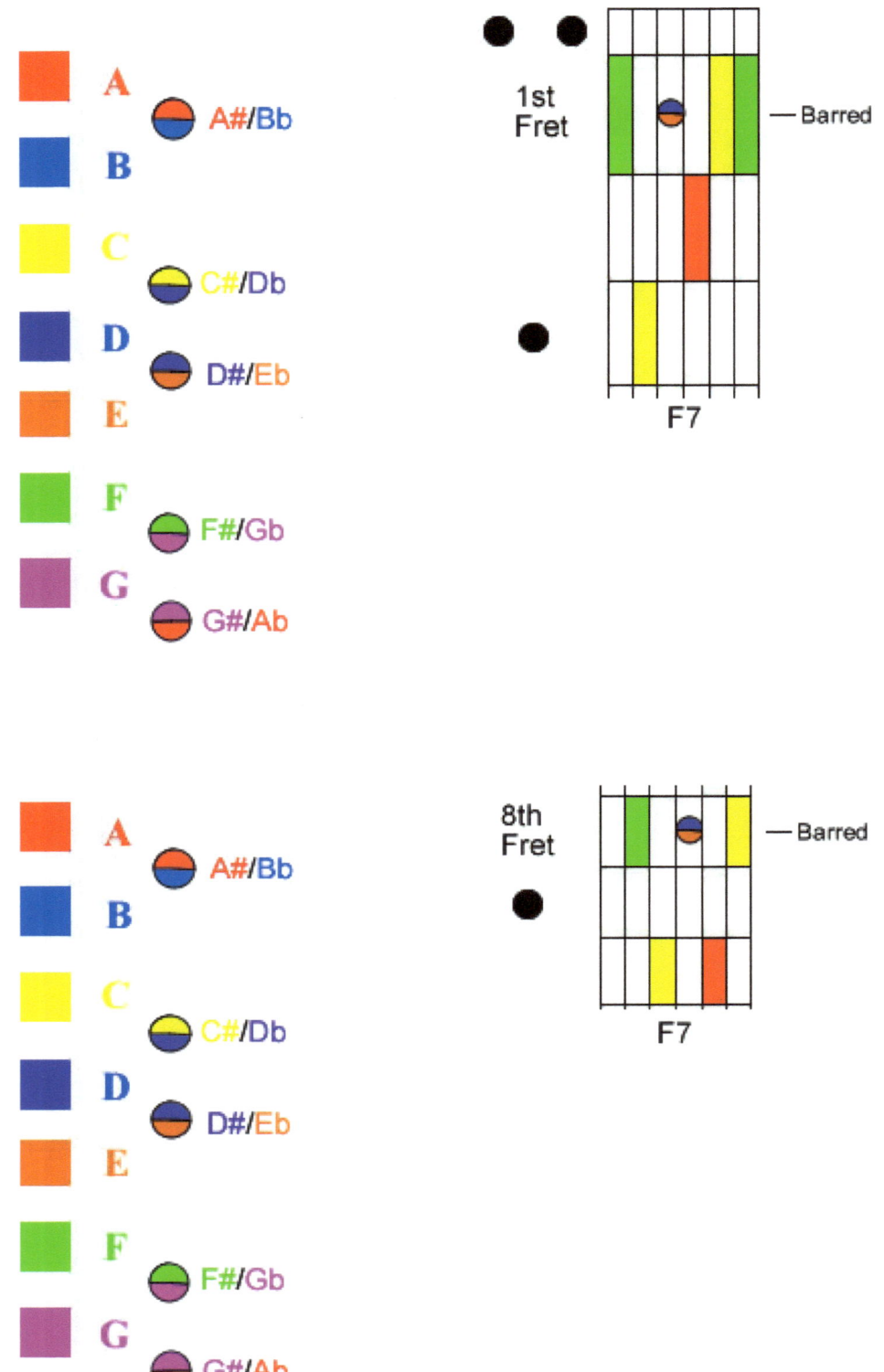

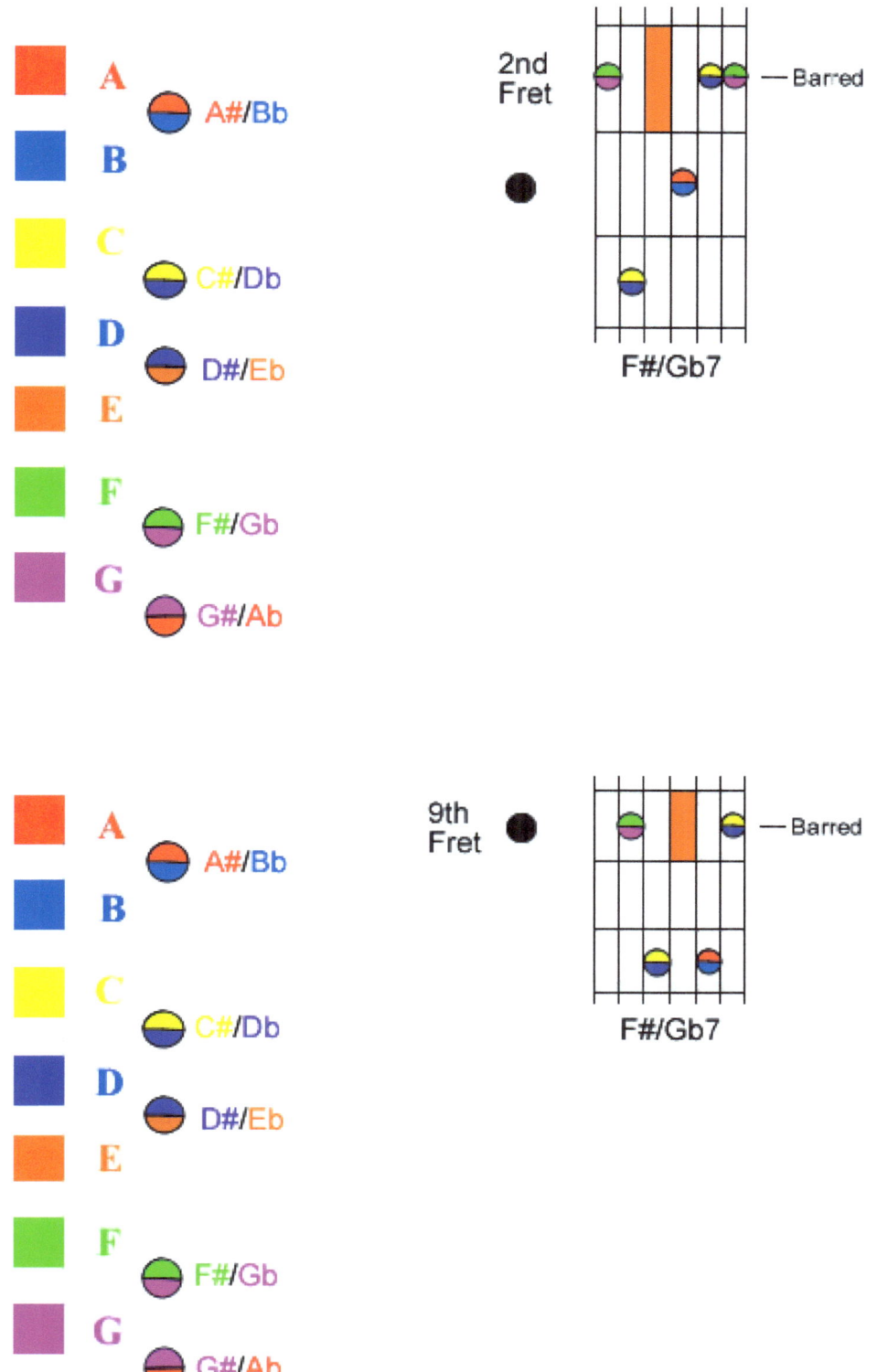

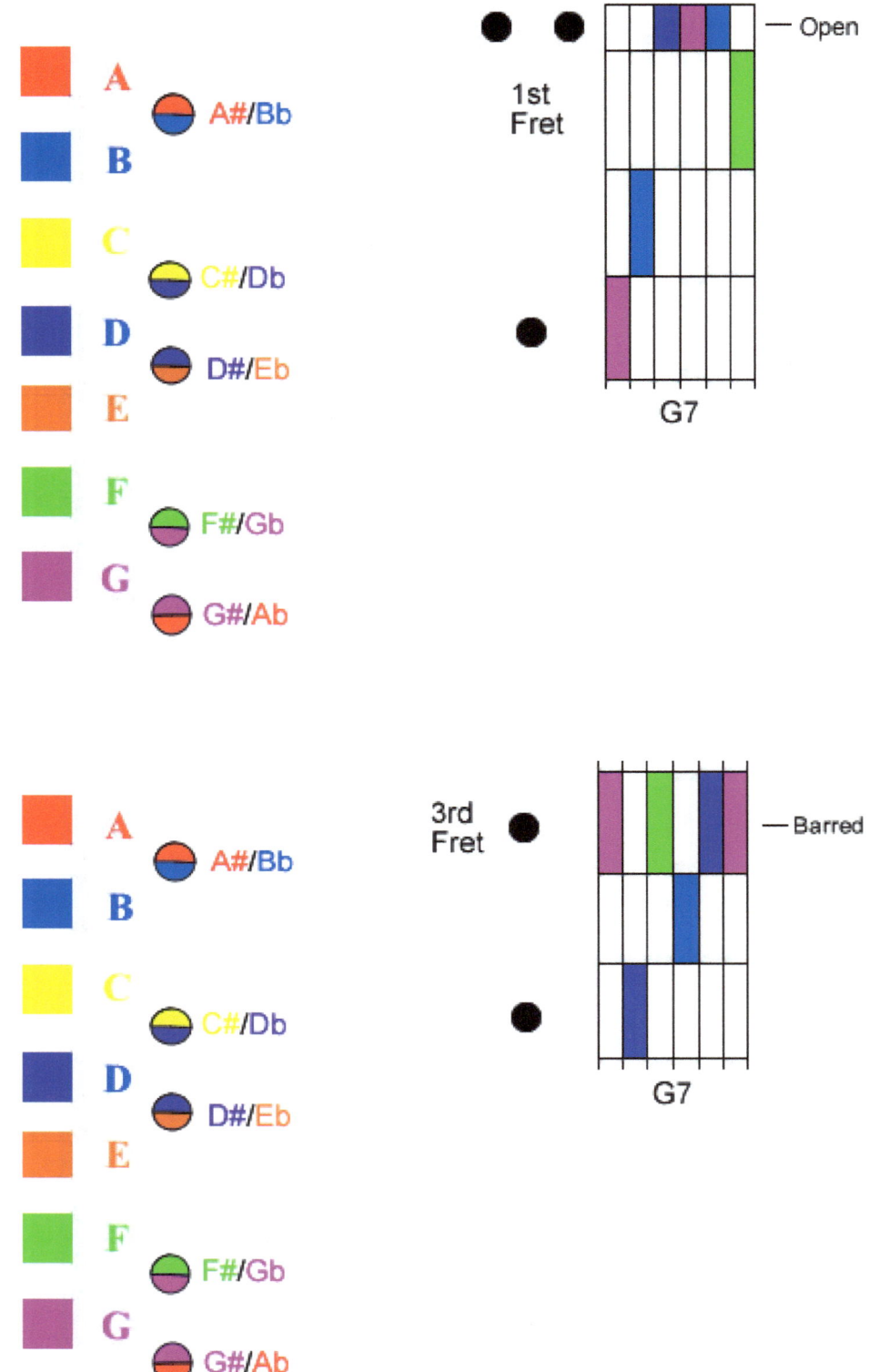

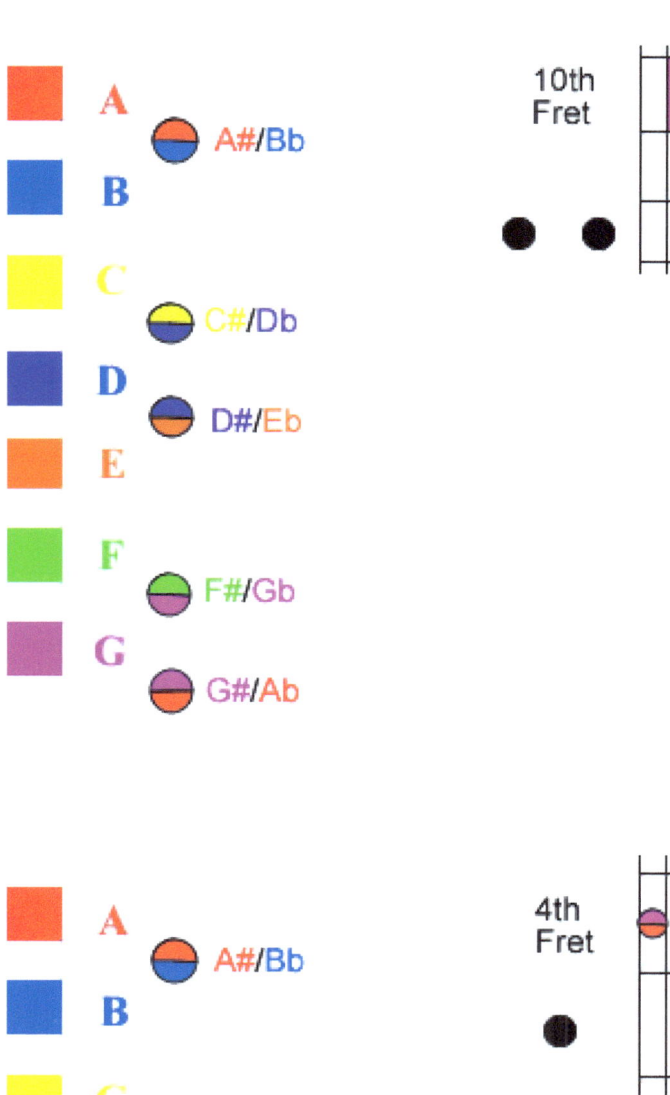
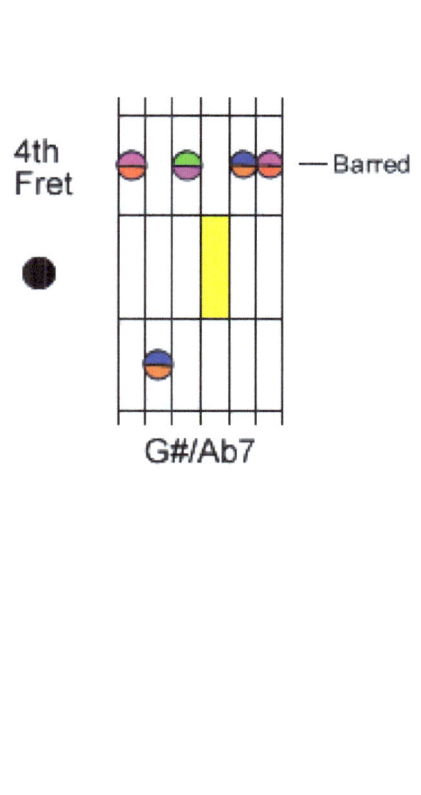

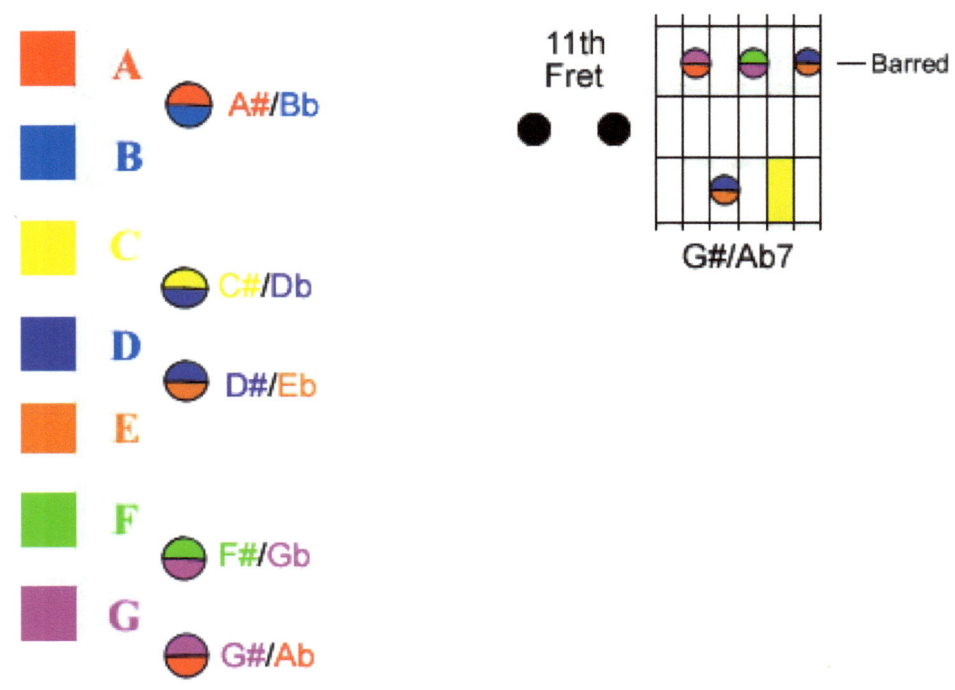

-Major 7th Chords-

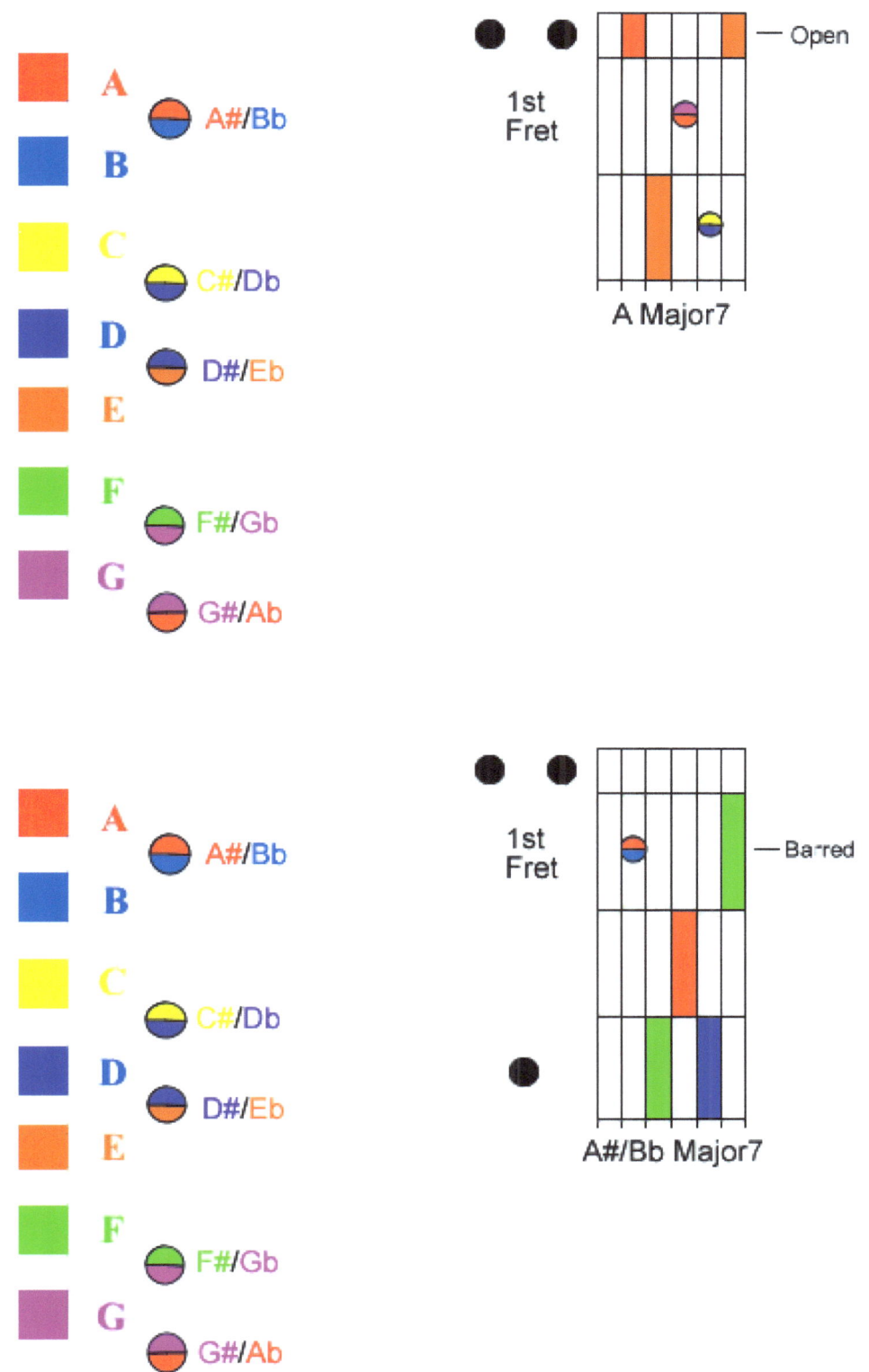

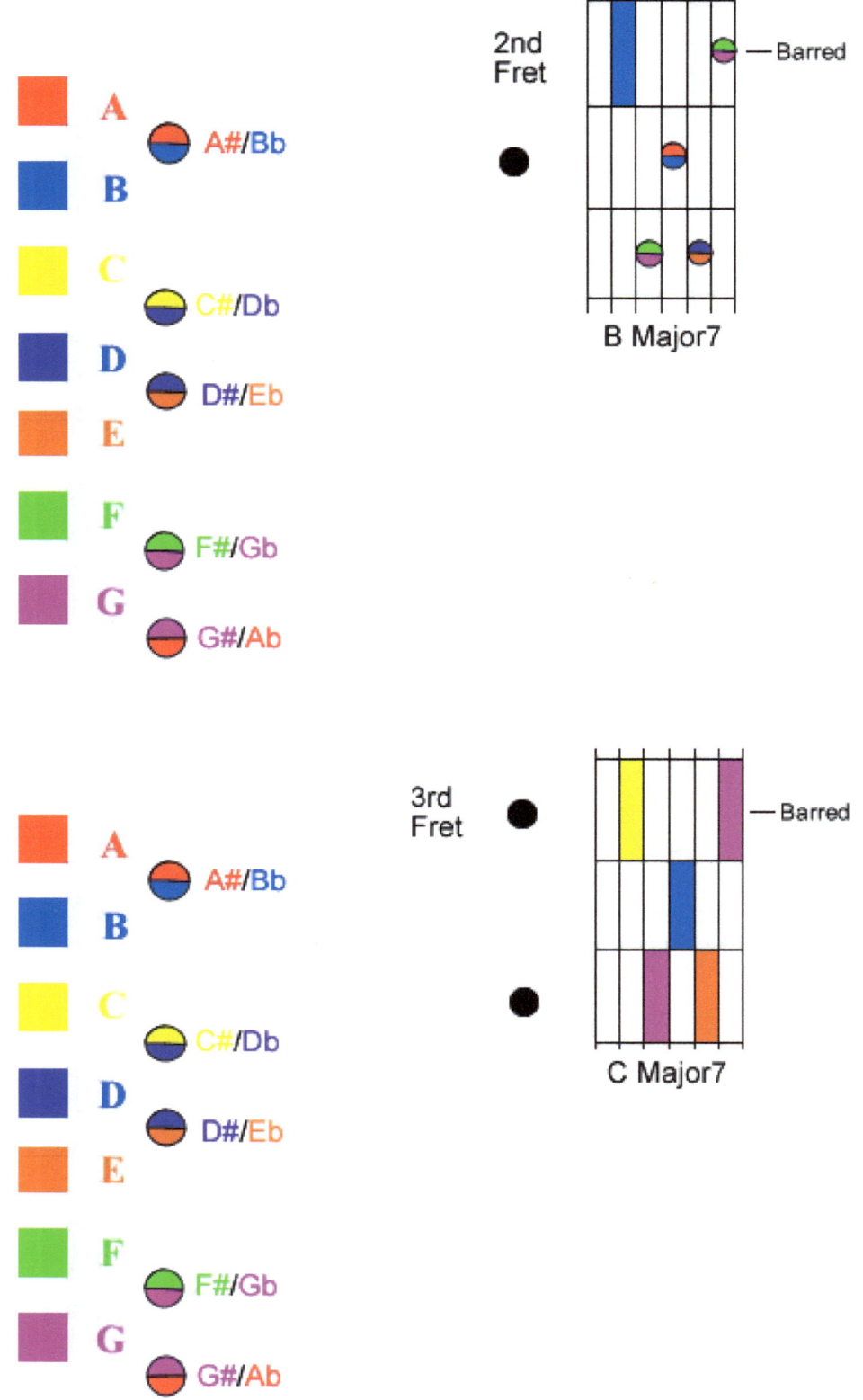

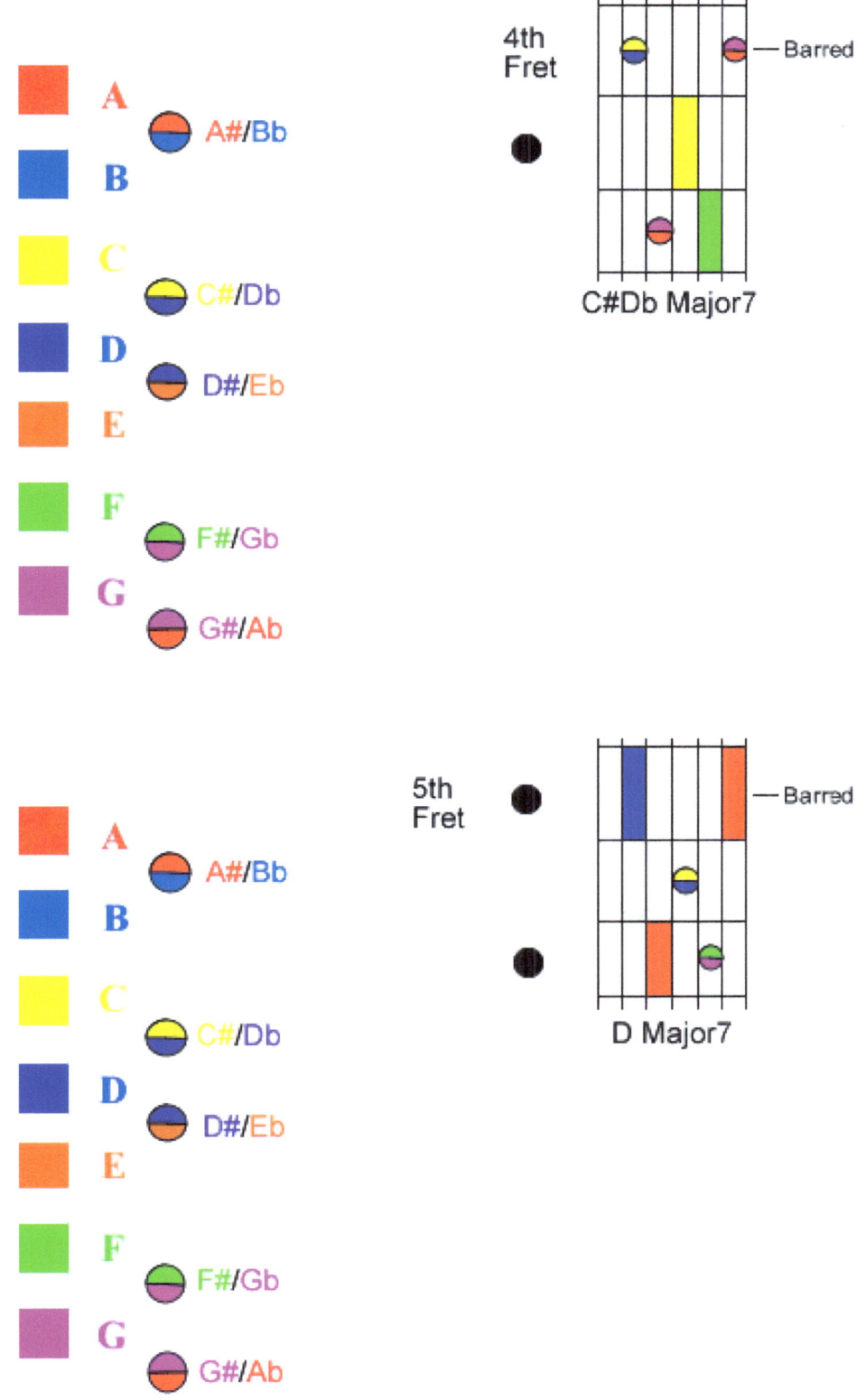

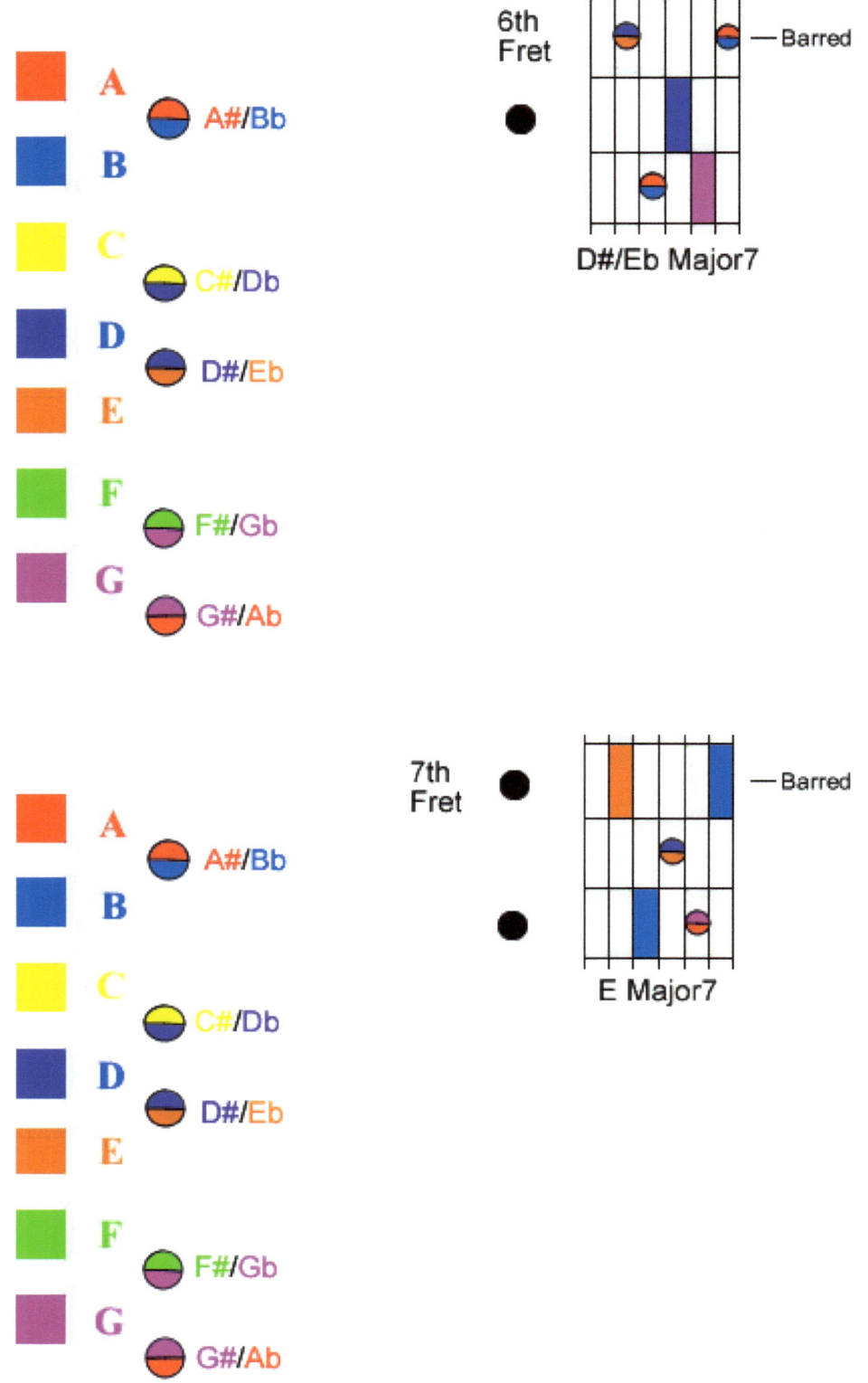

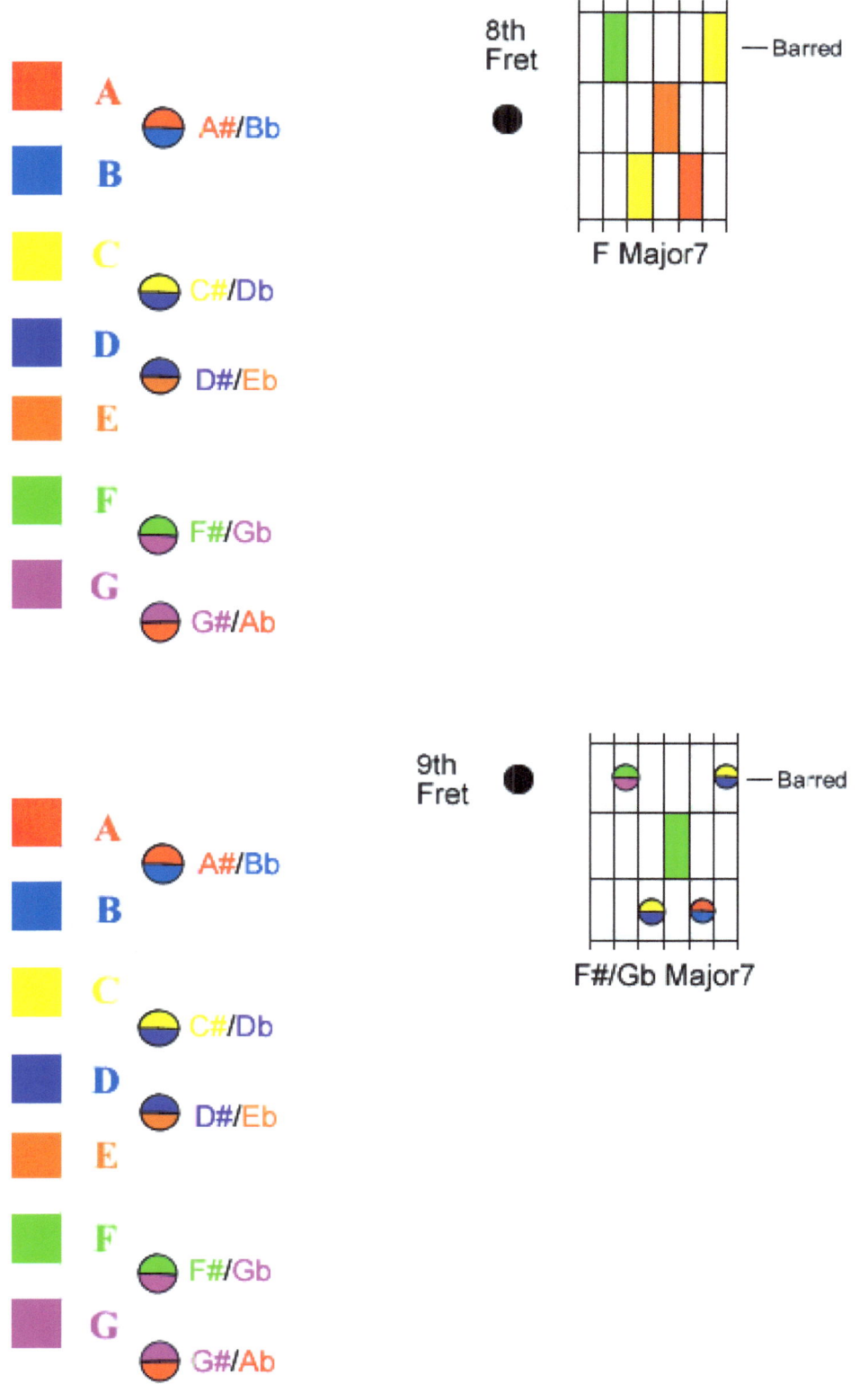

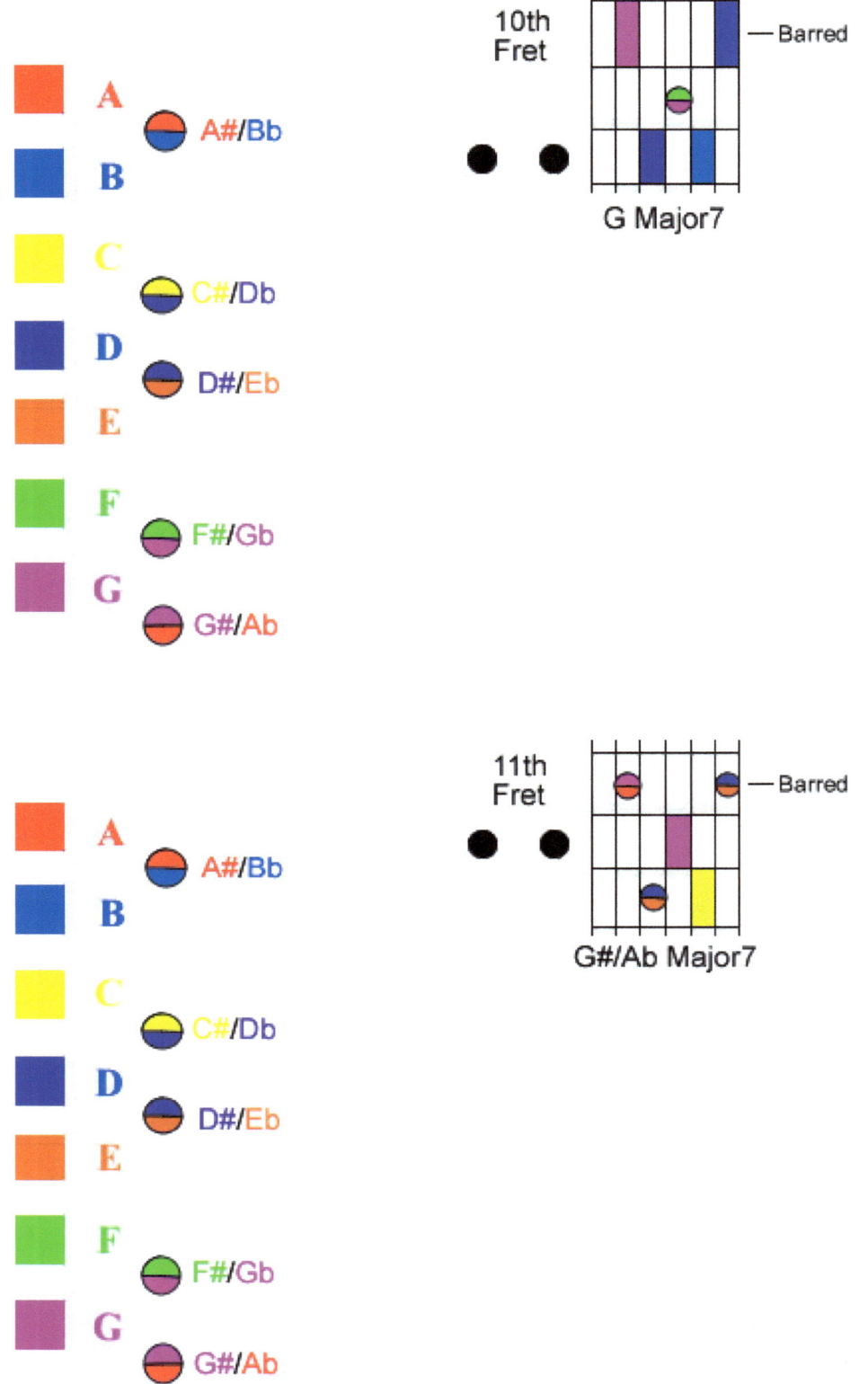

-Minor 7th Chords-

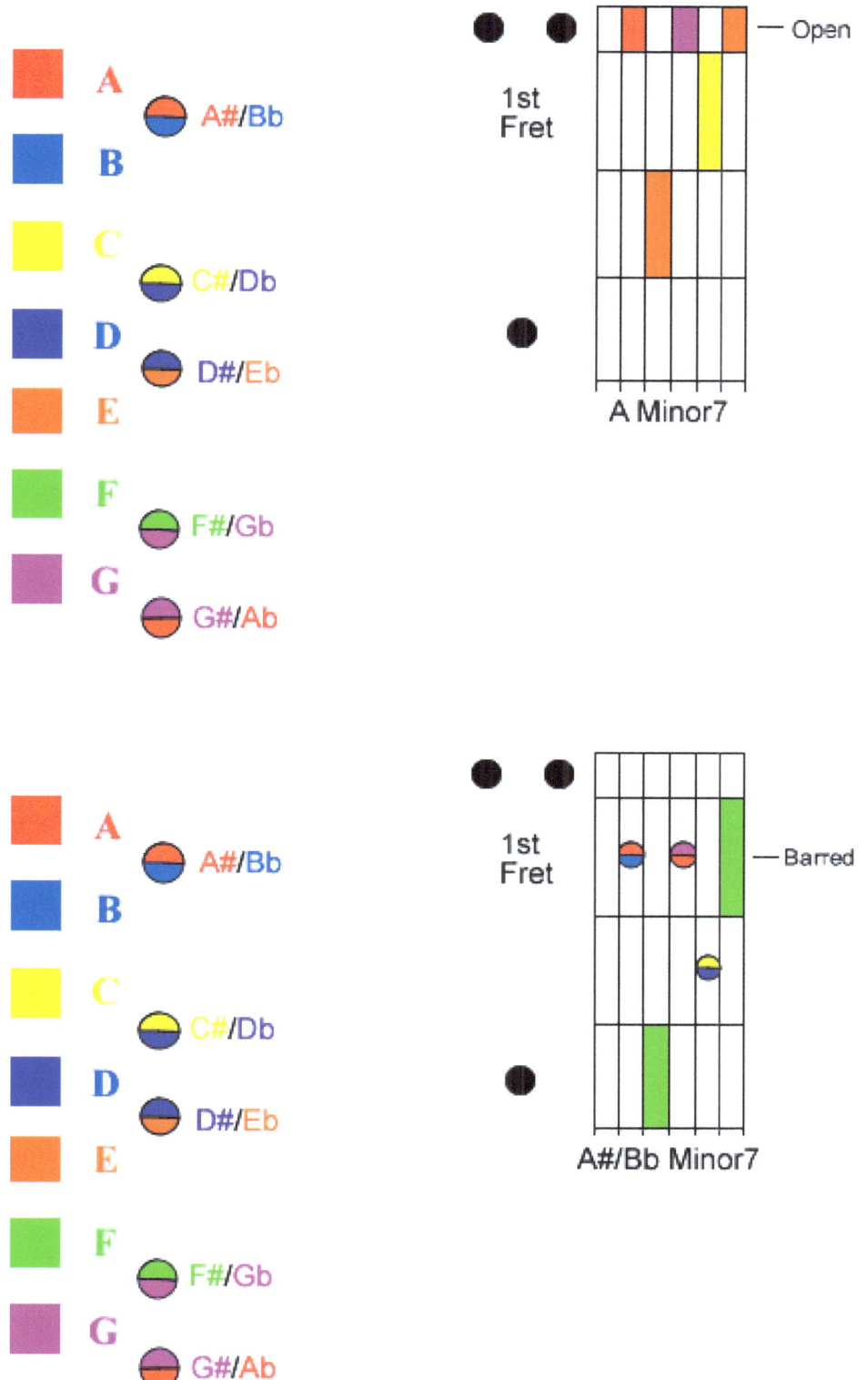

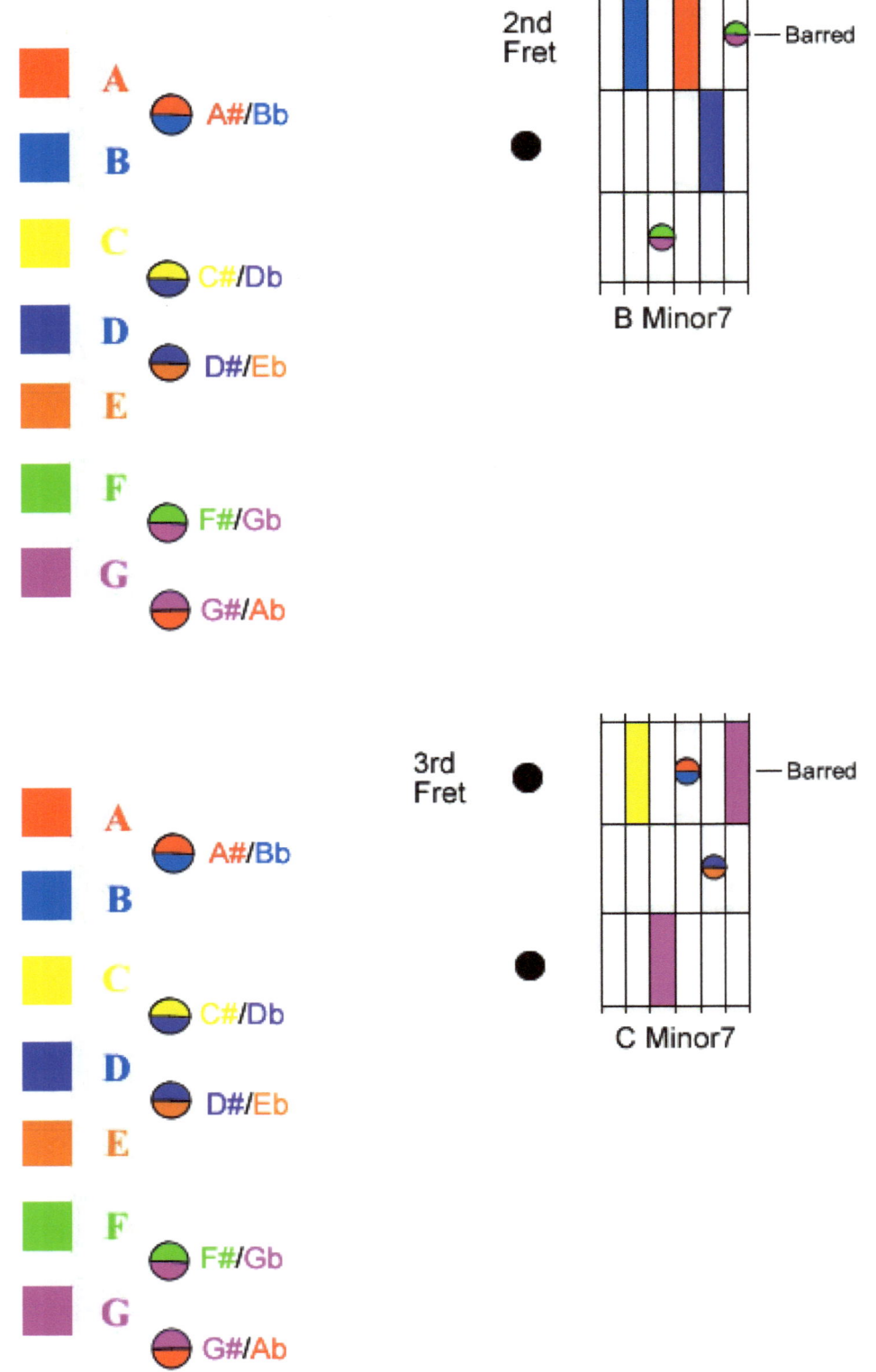

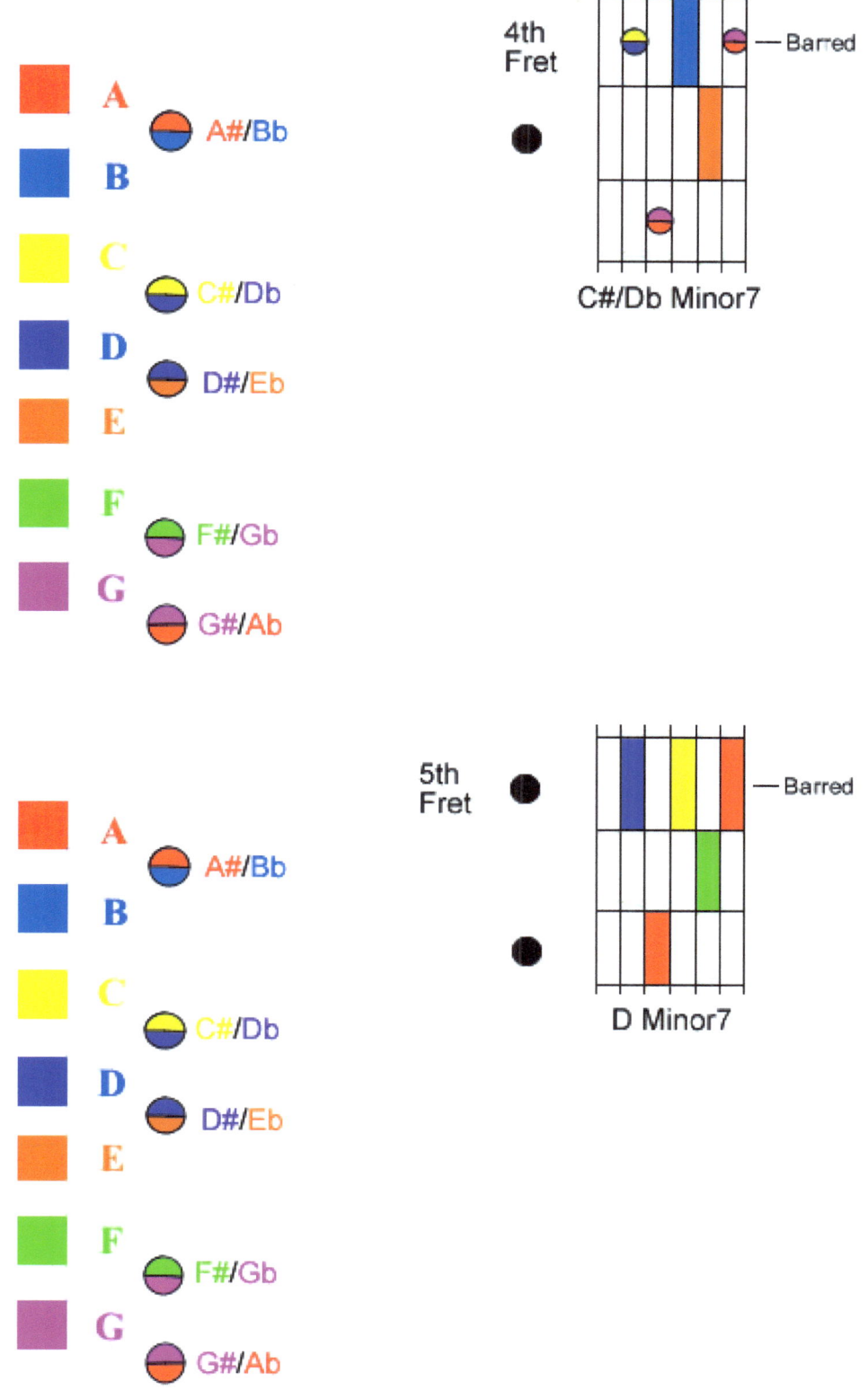

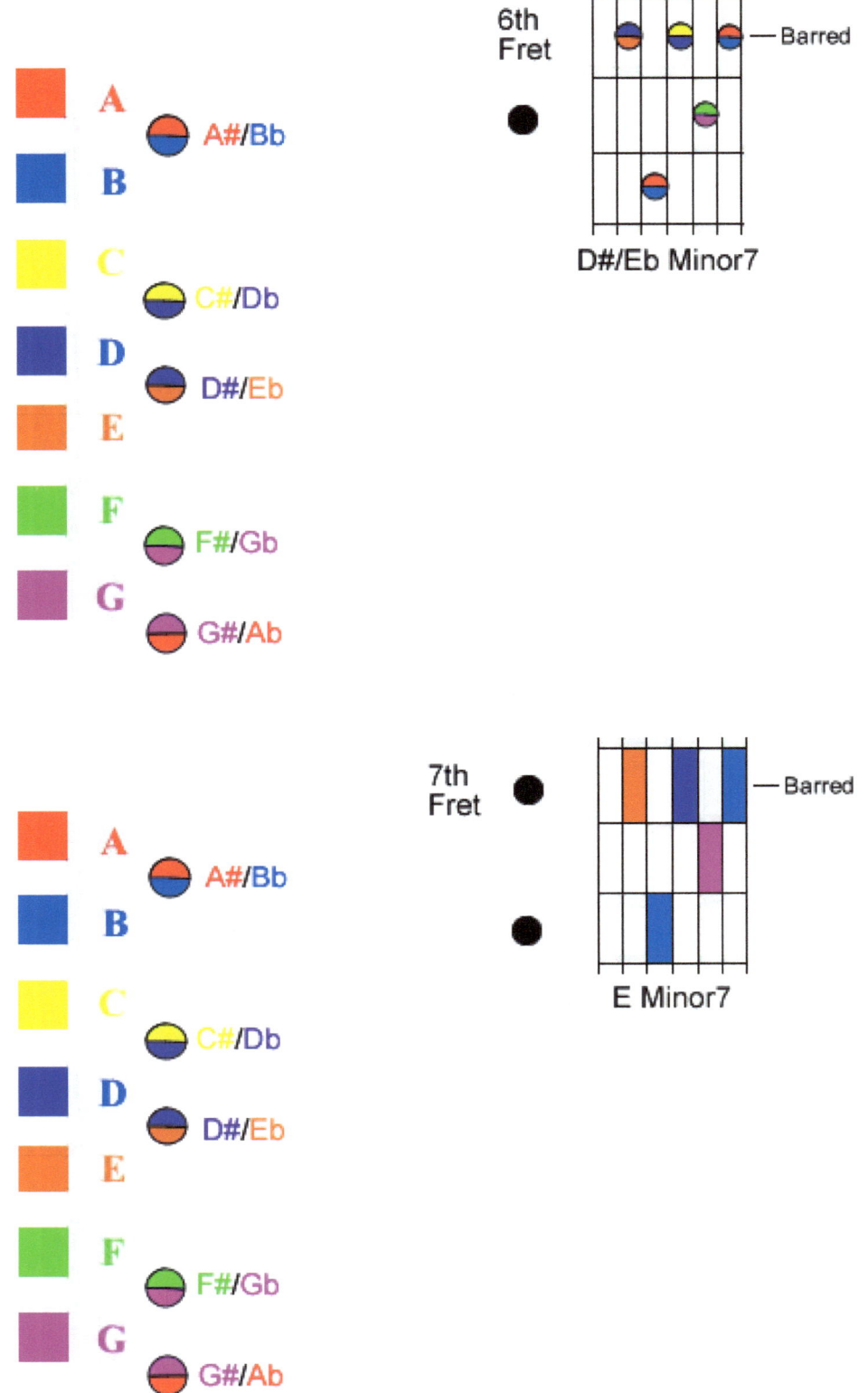

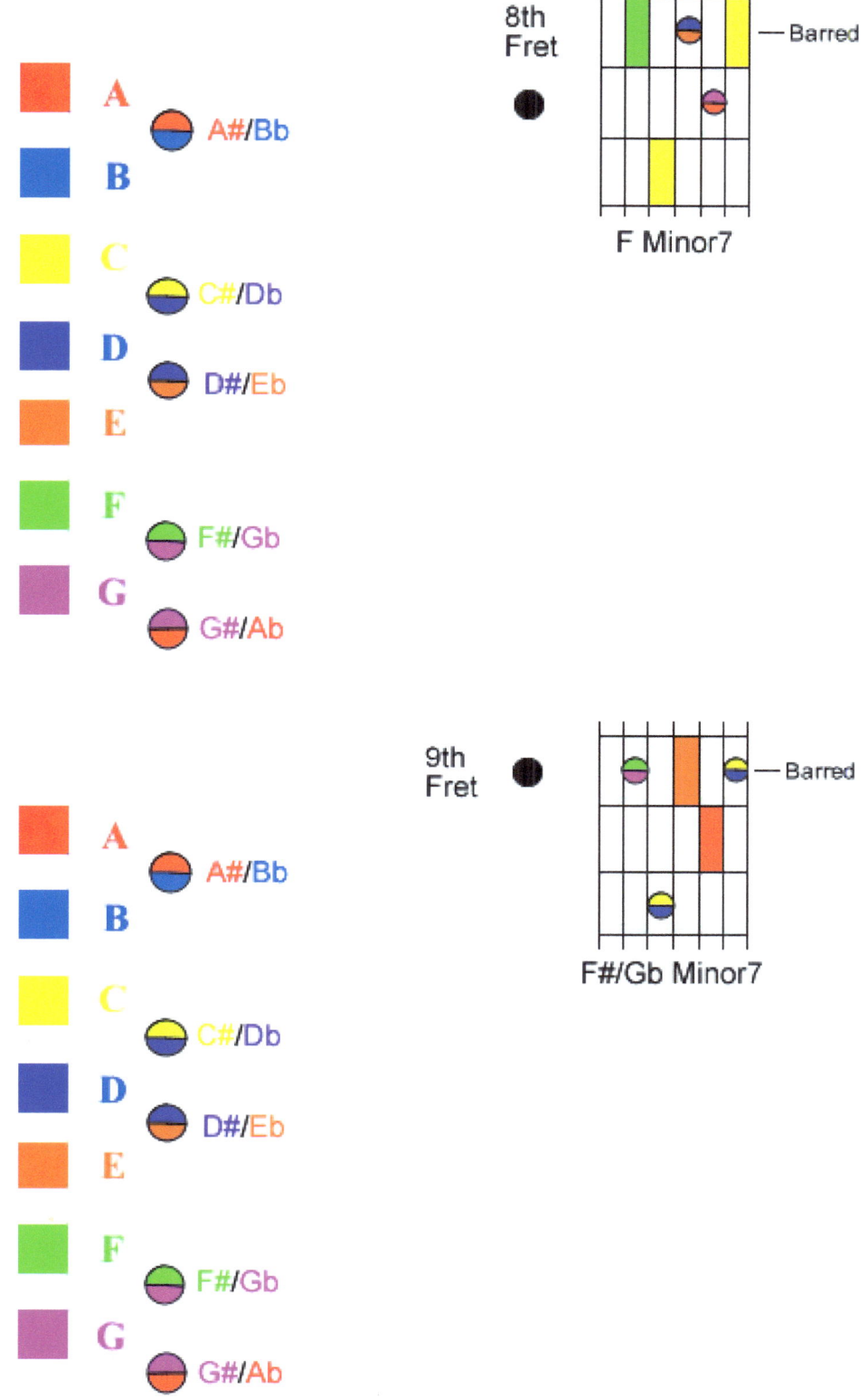

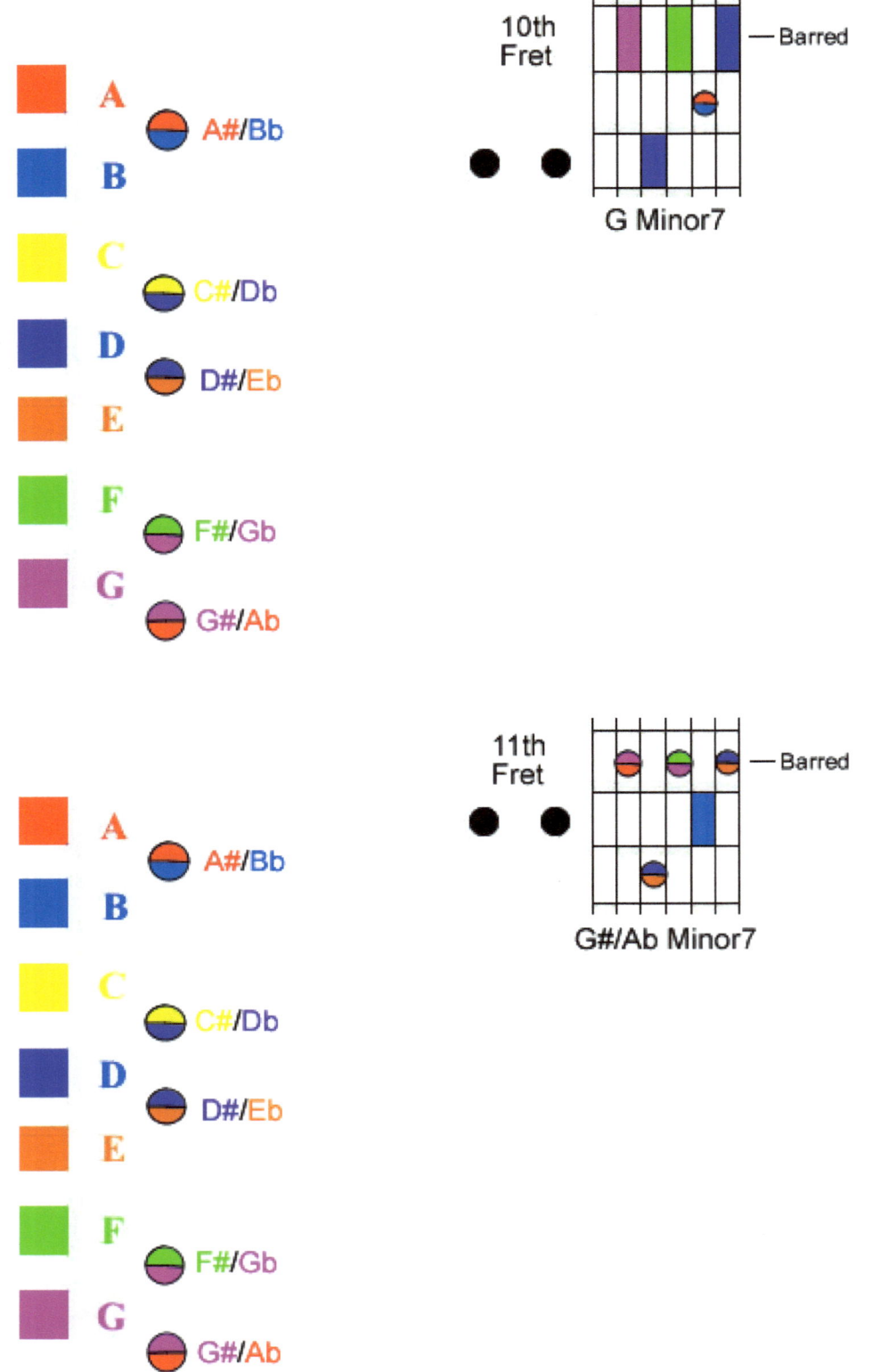